Contents

Foreword

Dr. Losoncy presents an extraordinarily high powered and comprehensive recipe for achieving success in all areas of life. He has taken the best from the world's great positive thinkers and combined it with his own years of exhaustive research on the subject of success. The result is dynamite!

The key to success, or achieving the goals you set for yourself, is a positive self-image. The first two chapters firmly convince the readers of their need for "self-image modification." The remainder of the book adroitly explains how this modification is accomplished.

Unlike any other book you have read, there is no attempt at creating obscure therapeutic models, and it may prove the most all-inclusive, pragmatic book on personal problem solving ever written. The author tells it like it is. He speaks from personal experience and a lifetime devoted to ferreting out the exact elements that distinguish the success from the failure.

Never have so many excellent techniques been presented in one book. Dr. Losoncy is a master at understanding the power of positive suggestion. He weaves a fabric of positive strategies so tightly, success appears failsafe.

Refreshingly, there is no claim that the methods described are foolproof. Success is still up to you. The point is well made from the beginning that the benefits to be derived from the described methods are "determined by your expectations." You will get only as much as you expect.

However, I would say that one would be remiss in not expecting a great deal from reading this work. I am thoroughly convinced of its merit. I've spent many years reading manuscripts professing to have the keys to success. This one comes by far the closest.

Think Your Way to Success is "not for a one-time reading, but for a lifetime." It gets you to ask questions about yourself and probe your belief system in ways you'd probably never considered before. It helps you to see just how much YOU ARE WHAT YOU THINK.

THINK YOUR WAY TO SUCCESS

How to develop your positive self-image
to achieve your goals and become
the person you want to be

Dr. Lew Losoncy

Foreword by Melvin Powers

Published by
Melvin Powers
WILSHIRE BOOK COMPANY
12015 Sherman Road
No. Hollywood, California 91605
Telephone: (213) 875-1711

Printed by

HAL LEIGHTON PRINTING COMPANY
P.O. Box 3952
North Hollywood, California 91605
Telephone: (213) 983-1105

Printed in the United States of America
Library of Congress Catalog No: 82-050851
ISBN 0-87980-396-7

The role of personal attitudes and feelings toward life in general take on new meaning as get-to-the-heart-of-the-problem techniques reveal why your world presently is as it is. The world is your creation. The author astutely points out that while we are influenced by our environment, we also have tremendous power to influence back—to mold our own environment.

New ways of reacting to and dealing with everyday events are continually pointed out. What is so amazing is the enormous ramifications a different way of viewing things can produce. Dr. Losoncy is an admirer of rational emotive therapy which places emphasis on the fact that it is not the event but the way you react to an event that determines your reality.

Attitude alone can determine your fate. The author conducts many intriguing interviews to determine differences between the ways failures and successes view the world. One particularly interesting finding was that "failures tend to believe that people become successful because of things outside of themselves." People who don't take responsibility for what happens to them seldom experience success.

That success can be *made* is the central issue of this book. If it couldn't, all the pointers and graduated sequences for improvement would be worthless. Regardless of education, background, and even ability, you can achieve your goals *if* you go about it the right way, starting with belief in yourself. That is pretty astounding news!

Beyond the positive self-image, much emphasis is placed on goal-setting. Deciding what you want and sticking to it gives focus and purpose to otherwise aimless lives. But no matter how glittering the goal, you must have THE PLAN, a method of achieving it. You must also have the fortitude to devise other plans should the first one fail. Dr. Losoncy warns against being too much of a perfectionist, i.e., being so afraid of making an error that you never even try. In the tradition of the masters of the East, the author holds to the view that the only fatal mistake is that which keeps you from ever trying again.

Action, therefore, is the vital key to all success. Positive self-image, goals, and plans are still so many castles in the sky until you manifest them in reality. "Reality is not what we wish it to be; rather, reality is what it is." A fine discussion is given warning against dwelling on what "should be." If you want something in life you *go for it!*

Dr. Losoncy does an excellent job of breaking down the illusions and myths that keep people from trying. Fallacies about the necessity of being "born" successful, coming from a good environment, or encountering few difficulties are quickly put to rest. He teaches you how to *expand* your self-image such that you expect more from life. Greater expectations lead to increased motivation, more energy, and more action.

The first of the seven skills for success that is fully developed involves unleashing creative potential. One of the ten steps to achieving this potential is to assume that every problem has a solution. I single this step out because it is so representative of the entire book. Dr. Losoncy simply does not believe in taking no for an answer. It is this unconditionally positive attitude that makes *Think Your Way to Success* so powerful.

Since it's all in the way you look at things, much attention is given to the worth of enthusiasm in making your dreams come true. Methods of developing enthusiasm in yourself and others (a good leadership quality) are extremely well delineated. This motivational section of the book alone makes it worth reading.

There are many more excellent techniques explored in this book, but rather than elucidate them, I'll let you get on with it to see for yourself. Personally, I found that the longer I gave to digest the material, the more relevance it seemed to have. Quotes, advice, and aphorisms would come to me apparently out of the blue when the context was relevant. It was like having a built-in automatic success guide.

May you have the same positive experience reading this book that I had. And may it always be with you! Good luck!

Melvin Powers

12015 Sherman Road
No. Hollywood, California 91605

Think Your Way To Success

Every human achievement started as a thought in the mind of a spirited individual who believed that the dream could be realized. Humanity has progressed from living in caves to climbing snow-peaked mountains that reach five miles high into the heavens, to living in satellites that soar proudly around the earth in less than an hour, and to wiping out diseases that have plagued the human body but not the human spirit for centuries. All of these achievements and more have been accomplished because of a few enthusiastic people with positive self-images and a desire for improvement.

Every single human problem has a solution. In fact, every problem has as many solutions as there are optimistic people who are willing to put their chins up and seek success. These are the rare people who have learned how to use their unlimited minds and think their way to success.

This book *is* a positive and practical approach to help you systematically build your self-image to achieve your goals and become the person you want to be. Start your trek to Success City today and take up permanent residence on the Street of Success by using the ideas in these pages—not for a one-time reading, but for a lifetime.

Think Your Way to Success by discovering the answers to these and many other questions:

What is the single most important factor in determining whether you will be successful and achieve your dreams? . . . .

Is there a formula for success? . . . .

What is the one question that you can ask a total stranger and know just by the answer whether the person will be a success or not? . . . .

How much of a role does luck play in bringing about success? . .

Are successful people born or made—or neither? . . . .

How could you expand your pool of romantic possibilities? . . . . .

Why do many people who are promoted to a new position, even though intellectually capable, fail? . . . .

Do you initially resist new positive ideas and belittle compliments about yourself? . . . .

Could you actually raise your intelligence and achievement levels just by changing one facet of your life? . . . .

How can you eliminate "I could never" or "I can't" from your vocabulary and go on to prove that "I can?" . . . .

Did you know that your current self-image is possibly totally inaccurate and that you may be underestimating your potential by miles? . . . .

What does your self-image have in common with a fortune teller? . . . .

How could you get that job you have always wanted? . . . .

Did you know you might have a "million dollar idea" in your mind right now? . . . .

How can you give yourself a refreshing, breathtaking view of life every day? . . . .

Would you believe that in ten minutes you can eliminate pressure, tension, and frustration from your life? . . . .

How can you get more "awake" time in your day? . . . .

Do you know how to turn negative unproductive conversations into positive productive ones? . . . .

Do you believe that every problem has a solution? . . . .

Have you ever made the mistake of not trusting your idea only to have someone else earn a promotion with the same idea? What can you do to make sure this never happens again? . . . . .

Why do some moderately talented teams beat other teams filled with superior talent? . . . .

How can you turn a "down-in-the-dumps" day around in a few minutes? . . . .

How can you write a positive, daily horoscope for yourself? . . . .

How can you become your own newspaper editor, write positive headlines for your future, and then let the success story of your life unfold? . . . .

How can you tell when your idea system needs a checkup? . . . .

How can you be an enthusiastic person whenever you want? . . .

How can you become your own optometrist and clear up your negative vision? . . . .

Are you living on Loser's Lane? How can you fire up your enthusiasm and move yourself out of this neighborhood? . . . . . .

Why is intelligence only a small ingredient in success and happiness? . . . .

Why is your attitude the most important ingredient in achieving success and happiness? . . . .

Who were Terry Fox, Irvin Westheimer, and Marva Collins? What can you learn from their experiences to turn barriers into achievements? . . . .

Why is it that when you become enthusiastic your self-image becomes more positive? . . . .

How does the vocabulary of I. M. Dull differ from the vocabulary of N. Thusiastic? . . . .

When was the last time you analyzed your good points? How can you learn the technique of being an Asset Analyzer? . . . .

Are you depressing or stimulating to people? . . . .

What are your claims to fame? How can you recognize the claims to fame in others to increase your popularity? . . . .

Do you suffer from the "in-my-day" disease? How can you overcome your affliction? . . . .

How much could you actually achieve in one day filled with enthusiasm? . . . .

How does a personal goal give you additional "lifting power?" . .

Do you have difficulty facing reality? How can you learn to face reality and negative inevitabilities and win? . . . .

Did you know that you are the Director of Environmental Engineering for the most important account in the world—your own? . . . .

You have heard the statement that you are a product of your environment, but have you realized that your environment is also a product of you? . . . .

What are the eight Positive Strategies you can use to make your environment work for you? . . . .

How do you issue a "cease-and-desist" warning to the negative thinkers around you? . . . .

How can you create a personal Advisory Board made up of the most positive people in the world to help you achieve success absolutely FREE? . . . .

Why haven't you ever seen a classified ad saying, "Nitpickers Wanted?" . . . .

Is it the little things, not the big things, that get to you? . . . .

How can you turn your negative emotions into positive productive ones? . . . .

What are the three most powerful insights necessary for you to achieve success and happiness? . . . .

Do you suffer from one of the worst diseases known to mankind—the Disease of Perfectionism? . . . .

What is the greatest gift that you could give yourself today? . . . .

How can you overcome your desire to be liked and approved by everyone you meet? . . . .

Do you at times live in the past and miss the power of the present? . . . .

How can you become an effective inspiring leader and motivator of people? . . . .

What are the six skills that effective leaders have? . . . .

How do you develop the talent of seeing perceptual alternatives in order to rise above any conflicts and find a productive resolution? . . . .

What are the secrets of building team spirit in your family, social group, or organization? . . . .

Does your body ever send SOS's—Sensations of Stagnation—to you? Do you ever look at your life and say, "Is that all there is?" What can you do to change that? . . . .

How can you overcome the problem of procrastination? . . . .

Are you ready to make that big decision to change your life? . . . .

What are the seven defeating factors of procrastination and how can you rise above everyone else by being an "on-the-goal-to-the-goal" type of person? . . . .

Are you intimidated by the "big" project? What technique can you use to attack it immediately? . . . .

Are you afraid to send meals back that aren't cooked the way you asked, always saying "okay" when you really mean "no," and generally allowing people to tread on you? How can you learn the sure way of getting what you deserve without hurting or angering someone else? . . . .

If you begin your trip to Success City today rather than tomorrow, you'll arrive a day earlier!

Acknowledgements

The music in this book, like the music in our lives, flowed from the orchestrated efforts of many people. The lyrics were primarily influenced by the writings of Alfred Adler, the psychiatrist of common sense, and Albert Ellis, the psychologist of reason. Prescott Lecky, the educator who saw the relationship between self-image and achievement, and Maxwell Maltz, developer of the principles of *Psycho-cybernetics,* played a powerful role in my "outlook" or "inlook." Finally, the ideas in *Think Your Way to Success* emerged from the most sensible book I have ever read, *The Magic of Thinking Big* written by David Schwartz.

The technical work for the symphony was completed by dedicated and competent persons. My incredible mother, Anna Losoncy, after not typing for 30 years, typed the initial draft. Her accomplishment humbled the achievement of the ant who moved the rubber tree plant. Next, talented Elaine Moyer typed almost nonstop to meet the deadline. W. David Berezen was "in tune" with the melody in my mind and completed the editing. Linda Kirn rounded out the lyrics with her proofreading skills.

On a personal note, I was inspired by Rose Bailey (see Chapter 1) who showed me that a disability doesn't have to be a handicap. The positive attitudes and encouragement of my father, Lew Losoncy, and my brother, Ron Losoncy, provided a constant lift. My publisher and personal friend, Melvin Powers, somehow or other, saw the completion of the symphony even before the first note was written. Henry Kirn, my enthusiastic associate, also conducted much of the research for the melody.

Finally, the energies to complete this symphony were ignited by the inspiration, enthusiasm, and fresh perspective of my loving best friend, Diane Love who taught me an important lesson—to live every day like it was your . . . first!

A Note To You From The Agreeable Author

Just before you read THINK YOUR WAY TO SUCCESS, let me take this opportunity to express unequivocally that "I agree with you." That's right! I can honestly say, without even knowing you, that I completely agree with whatever you believe the contents of this book can do for you. If you believe this book has nothing to offer you, that it is merely another one of those self-help books promising a lot more than it will deliver and that you are much too set in your ways to be changed by any book, then I agree with you. If these are your beliefs, then I assure you that this book will be of little value to you.

However, if, on the other hand, you believe that this book can help you fire up your enthusiasm, inspire a personal change for the better, and believe there is more happiness and success to seek and enjoy in your odyssey of life, then I agree with you 100%. The benefits you will gain from any written work are determined by your expectations.

So, either way, whatever you choose to believe, I agree with you. And since we agree, let's be friends.

ABOUT THE AUTHOR

Lew Losoncy is an international lecturer on encouragement, motivation, and communication. A TV personality, he is also a consultant to many organizations, including schools, hospitals, businesses, industries, and prisons, on how to improve morale. Dr. Losoncy has conducted workshops in over 40 states and in many of the provinces of Canada.

"Doctor of Encouragement," as he is referred to, is the author of many books, including *Turning People On, You Can Do It,* and co-author with Dr. Don Dinkmeyer of *The Encouragement Book: Becoming a Positive Person,* all of which are published by Prentice-Hall, Inc. He is also co-author with Henry Kirn of *How to Be Happy in Life Today,* published by Encouragement Associates in Reading, Pa., and founder of the ME Theory (*M*anagement through *E*ncouragement). Dr. Losoncy has developed a school of counseling, *Encouragement Psychotherapy,* described in the "Handbook of Innovative Psychotherapy," edited by Ray Corsini and published by Wiley Interscience.

Dr. Losoncy has been a counselor, college administrator, and professor of psychology at the Reading Area Community College. Currently, he is Director of the Institute for Personal and Organizational Development in Reading, Pennsylvania.

CHAPTER I

A Positive Self-Image: The Key Ingredient in the Recipe for Success

Success or failure! I know both of those words very well and, quite frankly, I prefer the former. At first glance, success and failure appear miles apart, but, in reality, the difference between a successful 30,000-day experience of life and a dissatisfied lifetime is a matter of only one factor!

What is that one factor that determines whether one becomes a success or a failure? To answer that question, allow me to introduce myself and share a little of my life with you. My name is Lew Losoncy, and presently I am a lecturer and author of books on encouragement, motivation, and positive attitude. Enough of my present for the time; permit me now to share a bit of my past. I was a high school failure. In fact, I recall quite vividly one point in my junior year of high school when I received five pink slips indicating that I was failing five out of my six school subjects. I remember the angry principal sitting me down in his huge, finely decorated office and asking me to explain the reason for my five F's and one D. I told him that my best guess why I had five F's and one D was that I was putting too much energy into that one subject! The good priest failed to recognize the humor in my answer.

My response really was not humorous. My failing grades were an unnecessary tragedy when, today, I realize that I had the potential for school success. Why then was I failing? Was I failing due to lack of

15

ability? No. Within a few years, I went to a university to earn a bachelor's, master's, and a doctoral degree and became a professor of psychology. So, lack of ability could not explain my school failure. Was I failing because of laziness or lack of motivation, as many of my teachers thought? No, because I was quite ambitious and read many books outside of school. Was my failure then a result of a poor background? Certainly not. I had two of the warmest and most encouraging parents that the world could offer. No, none of the usual reasons given to explain why people fail (such as inadequate ability, lack of motivation, or poor background) were accurate excuses for my failure. And, as the pages of this book unfold, I trust that you will become convinced that failure at school, on the job, or in any personal or professional relationship is rarely a result of inability, lack of motivation, or poor background. Instead, most failure stems from one source: a negative self-image.

I had a failure self-image. Because I had an image of myself as a person who could not achieve in school, I was destined for failure. The self-image is the ultimate blueprint for success or failure. With a failure blueprint, it is impossible to design a successful self-structure. The most powerful gift that I gave to myself was a positive self-image. This—a positive self-image— is the key ingredient in the recipe for success.

MY PERSONAL FAILURE LED ME TO CONDUCT SCIENTIFIC STUDIES OF SUCCESSFUL PEOPLE

Motivated by the personal experience of failing, I decided to delve deeper into the study of people who failed as well as those who were successful. I spent almost a decade and a half obsessed with discovering the answers to three key questions:

*First Question: Why do some people continually fail to set and achieve goals as they wander aimlessly through life?

---

*Please note that success is defined here as setting up and achieving goals. It is defined personally, and a successful goal for one person is not necessarily a successful goal for another. This book discusses ways of reaching physical, personal, social, emotional, recreational, habit-breaking, habit development, financial, professional, or spiritual goals.

My friend, the talented Carl Hausman, was a pianist for one of the most popular U.S. rock and roll groups of the 1960's. Despite touring throughout North America, achieving fame and glory, for Carl success was settling down with his wife and opening up a little ice cream store. Success is personally defined.

Second Question: Why do some people continually succeed in achieving their goals, loving to take risks, and turning trage-
dies into triumphs, thus enjoying life more?

Third Question: If there is a formula for success, can it be learned and
used by anyone? Will success be available to any-
one who learns the formula?

I concluded that if a recipe for success could be found and be under-
stood and employed by anyone, it would have powerful implications.
Using the recipe for success could mean the difference between happiness and unhappiness, between optimism and pessimism, between financial success and failure, and, maybe, between a fulfilling life and a
dissatisfying existence. Perhaps these ingredients of success could
even help a person suffering from ulcers, depression, hypertension,
migraines, or anxiety to experience a symptom-free life. Could using the
recipe for success possibly mean a longer life expectancy for people?

Yes, helping people to learn how to be successful was, for me, the
greatest challenge since Ponce de Leon's search for the Fountain of
Youth. My 15-year search for these secrets of success drove my inquir-
ing mind and spirited heart through the pages of thousands of books on
psychology and hundreds of thousands of miles of travel throughout the
world. In these travels, I served as a consultant to business, industry,
government, hospitals, schools, and even prisons. These experiences
gave me an opportunity to observe the thinking of successes as well as
the thinking of failures. I interviewed some of the country's top executives, salespeople, managers, teachers, clergy, physicians, and politi-
cians. I spent numerous hours listening to people plagued with depression, existential anxiety (the loss of meaning in life), paranoia, phobias,
and manic depression. In this book, I will relate interviews with people
who, despite physical disabilities such as cerebral palsy, mongoloidism,
or limb losses, achieved success. I listened intently to thousands of
successes and failures of persons from many different cultures, trying to
discover their achievements.

And I have great news! I have found some answers to why people fail,
why people succeed, and to the main question, "Can success-thinking
be learned?" Let me say jubilantly at this point that the results of my
studies demonstrate loudly and clearly that a success style can be learned
and a positive self-image can be developed by anyone. This book is a
discussion on my findings, and it is written with one purpose in mind—to
help you succeed in reaching those goals you want in life. I'll begin by

sharing some experiences that enlightened me as to the powers of a positive self-image. Stay with me and experience personally the unravelling of these incredible insights on success as the insights revealed themselves to me.

INSTANT FAILURE TO SUCCESS-THINKING OVER LUNCH

This book has been a long journey for me. My ideas and original theories changed drastically in the process when they didn't stand up to eye-to-eye confrontation with the facts. Very frankly, my belief at the conception stage of the research was that the most important difference between success and failure was probably a combination of luck and fate. That belief is quite common among lay people and, at first glance, one can see why. Isn't it true that luck allows some people to live longer than others? And isn't it a fact that some people are born into multimillion-dollar family businesses, while others are reared in the ghetto and are total strangers to opportunity? And even on an everyday scale, isn't it accurate that some people can eat all of the food they desire and never experience a partition bulge, while others seem to advance toward the rotund state just by the inviting aroma of food?

So, as a casual observer, my best bet was that the omnipotent boundary line between personal success and failure was simply a decision of life's lottery system. At that time, I was not alone in my theory that fate decided success. I listened to many other people (if not most people) of fatalistic foundations who eulogized their potential with pronouncements like, "You're born, you work, you die, and that's it," or, "The rich get richer, the poor get poorer," or even, "It's not what you know, it's who you know," and so on, and so on . . . These helpless views of life, while seemingly somewhat shaped in gloom, in the long haul were comforting in that they "gave one permission" to accept a life of mediocrity on the plateau of the status quo.

Then one day, in a powerful experience, my fatalistic philosophy of life was challenged. The scene was a posh restaurant in the Big Apple where I sat humbly eyeballing the menu in search of the cheapest entree. I was earning $5,100 a year, which is exactly what I was worth. Seated to my left was a group of obviously successful people sharing their personal portraits of life. As I listened to them, I became forcefully aware of the difference between their view of life and my own. Our contrasting views were even more apparent than the difference between their fine woolen clothing and my garden variety duds. One of the four gentlemen told how he grew up in the slums of Harlem, never knowing his parents. He was reared in a children's home and worked his way up the steep slope of success by taking one unpretentious job after another. Despite quitting high school to work at an early age, he knew he would return someday to finish not only secondary school, but also to earn a college degree in English. He realized that it would be difficult to re-enroll, but the vision of his positive personal destiny was implanted firmly in his mind. He eventually graduated from Columbia University. As more of the conversation unfolded, I discovered he was currently a vice-president of a major New York City publishing company.

Sharing his success story elicited similar thoughts from another of the four people. The second man, a deep-voiced man in a three-piece suit, described some barriers that attempted to put detours along his road to success. Although barely five feet tall, this gentleman expounded on a positive philosophy of life. He explained how he was denied his first few sales positions because of his height, and discussed the practical problems his size presented. In one instance, he was informed by a personnel manager that a tall salesperson subconsciously conveyed a more important message than someone smaller, and he was encouraged to seek employment in an alternate profession where size wouldn't be a major factor. On another occasion, he was told by a salesperson that sitting on a cushion (to elevate himself) while driving a client to dinner would surely detract from the respect so necessary to successful selling. As the three gentlemen listened intently, the well-groomed philosopher admitted developing a sense of stoicism regarding the problem of his size. He said, "I looked at myself in the mirror and concluded that it was a fact that I was small. And although I realized that there was little that I could do about my height, I was in total control of how I reacted to it. Sure, I could roll over and die and blame life for my size, but where would that get me? Certainly I would never become a millionaire that way. So I lifted my head up into the air, threw my shoulders back, and decided I would learn everything I could about the sales profession. The seeming importance of being tall was primarily in my mind, and when I took charge of my thoughts, my life changed. I made myself intellectually taller." I listened to the gentleman like a six-year-old with a dream of playing professional baseball would listen to Pete Rose—with my full attention. I learned how his philosophy of success was different from my previous idea that success comes from fate, luck, or a combination of both. His philosophy differed from mine in another way as well. His worked!

The waiter arrived. I glanced through the menu and ordered the most expensive filet mignon on the menu. The objective view of myself was changing. The sun was peeking its smiling face through my cloudy vision of life. I realized that my previously passive, hopeless outlook on life had been influenced by a biased sample. I had listened to people who were down and out. My previous ideas on life (that luck creates success) had come only from a limited few. No wonder the individuals I listened to were unsuccessful. They created a picture of life that was dark and gloomy. In their dim view, they concluded, "I can't change things because this is the way things are, and that's that."

So, my early outlook on life was influenced by people who basically felt helpless and handed the steering wheel of their lives over to fate. They chose to be backseat drivers and, as backseat drivers do, only complained when the car didn't go where they wanted! This restaurant experience was a shift for me. I was now listening to a new sample—four successful people who had taken hold of their life reins, had set up goals, and had driven over the sometimes bumpy, sometimes smooth, road of life to reach those goals. I lifted my chin to twelve noon and looked up for new experiences with more successful people.*

PREDICTING SUCCESS OR FAILURE JUST BY ANSWERING ONE SIMPLE QUESTION

That cafe experience inspired me to explore microscopically how the attitudes of successes differ from the attitudes of failures. To start your own journey on the road to success, I urge you to try one of the same experiments I conducted. If you experience similar results, it will have more of an impact on you than if you just listen to my findings.

Try to discover how differently people who are a success or a failure view life. The experiment is so simple that it is incredible. First, think of five people whom you would consider to be less than successful. Remember, a successful person is defined as a person who sets up goals and tends to achieve those goals. Select five people who appear to be going through life either aimlessly or who talk about goals and tend to procrastinate or give up before realizing their dreams. After you have composed your list of five people whom you feel have not been successful, think of five people who are. Record their names in your survey. After recording the ten names, you are ready to begin your experiment, which is a simple interview.

---

*Incidentally, I would suggest you start doing the same. In Chapter VI, Designing a Positive Environment to Work For You, specific ways of creating an encouraging environment are discussed. Your social environment plays a crucial role in your journey to Success City.

To make your experiment scientific, it is important that you ask all ten people the identical question. If the failures tend to answer the question with different patterns than the successes, you have discerned a potential outlook that separates success from failure. Now, here is the question that goes to the very heart of how success-thinking differs from failure-thinking.

Ask all ten of your sample subjects, "How much of a role do you believe that luck plays in making a person successful?" Please record all ten answers so that you can scientifically analyze the patterns in their responses. Again, it is vital for you to conduct this experiment so that you can personally experience the power of a person's attitude on success and failure.

Until you get your results, allow me to share some of the responses I received from my own interviews. I have conducted this experiment with the same question to a few hundred people. My sample of respondents included corporation executives, salespeople, teachers, hairdressers, managers, prisoners, clerks, mental hospital patients, as well as many other individuals. It is important to survey a complete cross-section of people. Here are a few of the comments I received:

"Luck is everything. . . . You just have to be at the right place at the right time." (Response from a male, age 27, unemployed for three-and-a-half years. He has not filled out a job application in two years.)

"The cards of life are stacked against you if you don't have money." (Response from female, age 36, former salesperson who recently lost her position for reasons of poor performance, missed appointments, and deception on expense reports.)

"Some people just get all of the breaks in life, others don't." (Response from male, 19, recent college dropout.)

As I analyze these three remarks, I see that each of the three respondents gives luck or fate the key role in determining whether success or failure happens. Perhaps your interviews will yield similar responses from people who are failing at life.

Next, I have recorded the responses of three people whom I classified as successful:

Q.   How much of a role do you believe that luck plays in making a person successful?

A.   "You make your own luck." (Response from female, age 32. She recently received an award for being one of the top ten teachers in the state of Pennsylvania.)

A.   "It wasn't luck that I have not missed a single sales appointment in the last two years. It wasn't luck that I made sure every single order I received from customers was promptly filled out. It wasn't luck that I made it my business to take at least four sales training or motivation courses each year. It wasn't luck that I went back to school in the evenings and in less than eight years earned a bachelor's degree in business. In fact, it wasn't even luck that my shoes were shined and my shirts were spotless when I made my sales calls, come to think of it. No, it wasn't luck that made me the top salesperson in the company this year. And it won't be luck when I do it again next year." (Response from a male, age 39. He was the top salesperson for a major California-based beauty supply manufacturer.)

My favorite response to this question came from an author of fiction books. He described how early in his life he was discouraged from pursuing a career in writing by some "failure thinkers" who told him that it was impossible to get a book published unless you either had a lot of money or had an "in." His response to the question of luck on success was:

> I concluded that waiting for luck to come to me before I did something myself was as ineffective as looking at my reflection in a mirror and waiting for it to move first. A much more effective approach to get myself to move was to start myself moving. Something interesting happens. When I moved, my reflection in the mirror passively followed.

The attitudes of failures and the attitudes of successes became clear to me and, I trust, will become as clear to you when you analyze the results of your interviews. Failures tend to believe that people become successful because of things outside of themselves. These external factors include things such as fate (breaks), luck (superstitions), or even the stars. Consequently, when success did not arrive at their doorsteps, they spent their energies blaming the world for not giving them a break.

Successful people, on the contrary, tend to see achievement as a product of "something inside" of themselves. So, when these achievers did not immediately succeed, instead of blaming outside influences they turned to that "something inside," believed they could be successful, developed a new plan, and moved on to accomplish their new goal.

What is this "something inside" that the successful have but the failures lack? What is this missing link in the chain of success? Allow me to share two insightful experiences I had a few years ago to demonstrate what this "something inside" successful people is.

ROSE AND CHARLES

One of the most moving experiences I ever had occurred while I was employed by a small Pennsylvania college. One day, a 29-year-old woman with cerebral palsy arrived at our admissions office door in her wheelchair. Her goal was to attend college. Our interview with her was still in its initial stages when it became obvious that the girl's very serious speech problem made it almost impossible for a meaningful dialogue to take place. She had to repeat every phrase at least four or five times before we were able to intelligibly connect her utterances. When time and again we failed to understand her words, Rose's head would bend to the side, her face assuming grimaces that reflected her frustration. Patiently she would regroup her energies to try to speak again.

Not only lacking an ability to effectively speak, the young woman could barely read, and she could not write at all. She was truly deficient in most of the key skills necessary to achieve success in college. But in spite of all the odds, that "something inside" brought Rose into our admissions office with the goal of becoming a college graduate.

Rose was apparently unaware that the college was unequipped to serve her special needs. Unable to walk without assistance, how could she make it up the steps to the classrooms on the second floor? Lacking the fine coordination to write, how could she take notes? How would she be tested? Which professors would be willing to admit her to their classrooms and face the burdens and frustrations of dealing with her many special needs? Every thought that could sift through a narrow person's mind seemed to point directly to the conclusion that Rose was not college material and that the college was not prepared to help her climb her ladder of success.

Rose, however, had one asset that helped her soar over all of those mountains of obstacles. The singular but paramount asset was her belief that she could succeed. She had a positive self-image, the key ingredient in the recipe for success. Her self-image and the positive attitude that it gave birth to impressed the college admissions staff so much that she was given the green light to attend. After Rose was granted admission to college, a strange thing happened; the college people began to believe in Rose and, in their beliefs, they started to find solutions to deal with each of the barriers, one by one. One administrator even commented that he had seen hundreds of students with above average intelligence who did not succeed in college because they lacked what Rose possessed—a positive self-image and a belief that she could succeed. (Allow me to ask you whether you would prefer a brand new automobile in the middle of a desert with no gas in it or an older car with a full tank of fuel? Or would you rather have nothing at all except a tremendous belief and enthusiasm in yourself, or have everything with no hope or self-confidence at all?) Rose had a full tank of enthusiasm, hope, and confidence! She enthusiastically began her college career. Not long after Rose was admitted, I left that college position to work in a private consulting capacity. Consequently, I lost contact with Rose.

The years passed, and I almost forgot about her. However, I was invited to return to that same college to deliver the commencement address for the graduating class of 1980. As I watched the parade of graduates proudly march across the stage at the Rajah Temple in Reading, Pennsylvania, there appeared a little girl wheeling herself across the ceremonial stage. Yes, it was Rose. She was part of the parade of celebrants coming to reap her reward. She knew she could earn her college degree, and she did it. With no high school degree and no ability to write, deficient in her ability to speak, incapable of walking—all of these disabilities were not powerful enough to keep that "something inside," Rose's positive self-image, from achieving success. As I looked out into the thousands of mostly unknown faces, I saw them unite to stand to show their appreciation to Rose for the gift that she had given to them—a conviction that if you want something in life, go for it.

The importance of Rose's success story is magnified by the second experience that I had in the same city. Following a motivation workshop that I conducted with the agents of a real estate firm, one of the salespeople came to speak with me. The man, who appeared to be in his early thirties, extended his hand to me and initiated the following dialogue:

"Dr. Losoncy," he inquired, "do you remember me?"

Apologetically, I responded, "No, I'm sorry."

"I'm Charles——, and I met you about four or five years ago when you were the Director of Admissions at the Community College."

"Were you a student there, Charles?"

"No, but at the time I was thinking about attending college and studying business."

"And you eventually decided not to?"

"Yeah. You see, more and more I realized that it would probably be too tough. I mean, at the time I had been out of school for about four or five years and had forgotten almost everything I learned in high school. So I decided against going to school at that time. But maybe someday I'll spend some time rereading my high school books and go to college. But I know that if I went now and competed against those kids fresh out of high school, they would snow me."

As of this writing, Rose, the woman with cerebral palsy who lacked an ability to read, write and speak (but had a positive self-image), is counseling cerebral palsied people. Also, as of this writing, Charles, the high school graduate with a negative self-image, is unemployed and still looking for a belief in himself. Rose had a disability; she did not have a handicap. Charles did not have a physical disability, but had a mental handicap, or a negative self-image. Who was better off?

The key ingredient in the recipe for success, the "thing inside," was Rose's life inlook, her positive self-image. The reason Charles failed was not lack of intelligence, nor limited education, nor bad luck, but rather a negative self-image. The key ingredient in the recipe for success is a positive self-image.

Before proceeding in our discussion on how self-image leads to success or failure, it is important that a few misconceptions, or common myths about why people become successful, be laid totally to rest. What are some of these frequently heard reasons to explain success?

MYTHS ABOUT SUCCESS

Lay persons have many theories about how a person becomes successful. For the most part, these theories are inaccurate. And inaccurate theories about success, like inaccurate theories that the world is flat, need to be challenged by the adventuresome before climbing to the peak of success. Failures spend much of their time marketing three major reasons why they have not made it and why life chose to smile on everyone else. People living in "Loser's Lounge" become skilled at using a technique that psychologists call rationalization. Rationalizations are attempts to give "good" reasons or excuses for personal failure.

What are these three major myths or rationalizations that failures use to explain how people become successful?

Myth I   Successful people are born, not made.

Myth II   Successful people are developed in "good" environments and thus are a product of a "good" past.

Myth III   Successful people are those who faced fewer difficulties and fewer obstacles in life than failures.

Overcoming Myth I: Successful people are born, not made.

The belief that some people, at conception, are destined for success in life is, fortunately, in today's scientific world seen for what it is, i.e., an archaic excuse to explain failure as simply being the result of "life's frown." While at one time this belief was popular, the result of recent research has brought new facts into the sunlight. What are these facts that challenge the theory that successful people, by nature of heredity, are destined for success?

First, identical twins with the same genetic code have been found to differ significantly in their degrees of success. Remember, identical twins have the exact genetic code. If genes automatically produced success, both twins would achieve it. Second, thousands of people each year take leadership courses, enroll in success-oriented programs, read success books, listen to success tapes, and literally change lifetimes of failure into success. Success, in hitting a golf ball, dancing, learning math, or even kissing, can be learned, developed, and achieved regardless of genes or a history of failure.

Consider the examples of Rose and Charles. Genes certainly did not explain Rose's success and Charles's failure. Charles had more basic intelligence than Rose. Charles had a normal physical body and Rose had cerebral palsy. Yet Rose, with her positive self-image, overcame the obstacles. Charles, with negative self-image, failed. A genius with a negative self-image is at a disadvantage to a person with a positive self-image and average intelligence.

Myth II: Successful people are developed in "good" environments and thus are a product of a "good" past.

The argument that people become successful solely because of the way they were raised or where they grew up has more credence than the argument that genes automatically produce success. Psychologists have found that certain environments "tend to" produce certain behavioral patterns in rats, pigeons, cats, mice, horses, dogs, and many other animals. Even with humans, researchers in psychology have discovered that certain environments "tend to" invite certain behaviors. Yet these behavioral patterns are significantly less predictable in humans than in the lower level animals. The reason a human's response to his environment is less predictable than animal responses needs no explanation to anyone who has tried unsuccessfully to "condition" another person, or even has watched a three-year-old child in the process of creating something new.

The argument that people are totally a product of their environment can be disputed with the simple facts. The fact is that there has never been any psychological study (nor, if I dare stick my neck out on a very solid limb, will there ever be one single study) that shows a perfect relationship between a person's environment and the person's behavior. That is correct! Not one single study. Despite all of the credit that the environment receives for creating success or failure in individuals, research shows that environment, at most, can explain and predict about 30% of behavior. So, while it is true that how or where people were raised is a factor in success or failure, it is less than one-third of the total factor. In fact, in Chapter VI, Designing an Environment That Works for You, the point is made that you have more of an influence on your environment than it has on you.

Every graduation ceremony publishes lists of students who succeeded in college despite being raised in the most impoverished environments. By the same token, many children who are products of so-called "good" homes can be seen with very serious problems. So, while environment again "tends" to write certain successes and failures, environment by itself does not automatically cause success or failure.

Look again at Rose and Charles. Rose's environment surely does not explain her success, just as Charles' environment does not explain his failure. Rose had less than five years of a formal educational environment and Charles was a high school graduate. Charles's social environment consisted of many more broadening experiences than Rose's. He could drive from the Atlantic to the Pacific Oceans, if he chose to, on any given week. Rose, however, was socially limited by her immobility. So neither environment nor genes could totally explain why Rose succeeded and Charles failed. On this note, psychiatrist Alfred Adler concluded, "Do not forget that it is neither heredity nor environment that are the ultimate determiners of our personality. Instead both are only the building blocks or the raw materials out of which we construct ourselves according to our own creative style."

Myth III: Successful people are those who encountered fewer difficulties and fewer barriers than those who were failures in life did.

The British historian Arnold Toynbee concluded that humans cannot grow if life is either too easy or too difficult. Overcoming obstacles may be a necessary part of building the success muscles if the individual copes and chooses to weightlift the barriers. If, instead, the individual chooses to give up, a flabby failure-feeling builds around the will. Successful people differ from those who fail not in the lack of barriers, but in their belief that they can overcome the barriers and achieve their goals. Failures make excuses or give up when faced with obstacles.

During a difficult time in my life, I received a symbolic meter stick from a friend. On the measuring tool's surface appeared the words, "Trouble is opportunity in work clothes." The shrewd quote helped me to view my situation differently and to move ahead and overcome the obstacles that had stopped me a day before.

If you believe that successful people face fewer difficulties than failures do, you need not look further than Rose and Charles. Charles viewed the fact that he had been away from school for five years as a barrier and gave up. Rose, however, saw her difficulties, disabilities, and lack of academic preparation as merely an "inconvenience," not a reason to give up. Think of people you know. Are all your successful friends the people who found no obstacles? Even consider yourself. Were there times in your life when overcoming hardships actually made you stronger?

I recall another woman who, at age 61, sought admission to college. She had been away from school over four decades and already had been a grandmother five times. Were age and lack of preparation a reason to give up. Heavens, no, not for Josephine! With an excitement in her eyes, she enthusiastically proclaimed, "I'm looking forward to learning some new things. My hearing isn't as good as it used to be, so I bought myself a tape recorder. With the recorder, I can listen over and over again to the professor's words." With that attitude of success and her positive self-image (despite the barriers of age and hearing loss), I need not tell you that today Josephine has her college degree proudly displayed in her living room on the mantle.

When you dig deep into any success story and go beyond the surface, you find innumerable obstacles the individual faced and overcame. Henry Ford failed continuously in his early ventures. Walt Disney filed bankruptcy numerous times, and during some of his "crazy" schemes, Thomas Edison conducted experiments with negative results over 10,000 times. Johnny Unitas, perhaps the greatest quarterback of all times, could not make a professional football team in the beginning.

Talking about barriers, a peppy, young college girl named Carol Johnston set up a goal of becoming a gymnast on a university team. She was only 4' 11" tall—a barrier. Apart from her obstacle of size, she was blessed with only one arm—another barrier. Yet she worked towards her goal and pointed her "will compass" to success. Carol, like many other people when faced with an obstacle, could have easily given up, thrown her arm up in the air, and blamed the world, or even wasted her energies getting angry at people who have two arms. Not this petite mountain of inspiration! Carol concluded that having only one arm meant she had to work harder to achieve her goal. She turned her disability into determination.

DISABILITY + NEGATIVE SELF-IMAGE = HANDICAP

DISABILITY + POSITIVE SELF-IMAGE = SUCCESS

Competing against hundreds of other girls with two arms, she made the U.C.L.A. gymnastics team. Her success story does not end there. Carol Johnston went on to become one of the top gymnasts in the United States.

The theme of successful people might well be captured with the catchy phrase, "When life gives you lemons, make lemonade." Yes, the notion that life is always a bed of roses for successful people is as inaccurate as a saying that you can grow grain without rain. The obstacles that successes and failures face are often similar, but their reactions are different.

REACTIONS TO OBSTACLES

Responses from Failures or People with Negative Self-Images	Responses from Successes or People with Positive Self-Images
1. Complains—"Things should be easier."	1. Analyzes obstacles—"What are the problems?"
2. Excuses—"If only it weren't for this barrier, I could succeed."	2. Generates creative alternatives a. First, . . . b. Second, . . . c. Third, . . .
3. Blames—"Why me?"	3. Develops a plan from the best alternatives
4. Gives up—"What's the use, it's hopeless."	4. Acts
	5. Analyzes actions

FAILURES AND SUCCESSES

The failure (with a negative self-image) concludes, "I can't overcome," while the success (with a positive self-image) concludes, "The challenge is tough, but I can lick it." Always thank the positive person because with his or her help the whole world progressed, diseases were cured, and the moon was reached. Yes, the world has progressed only because of a FEW PEOPLE WHO POSSESS THE MOST POWERFUL GIFT OF ALL. That gift is not "success genes," not a "good" environment, and certainly not a past history lacking obstacles. The reason the world has progressed is because of a few people who used the powers of their positive self-image. A positive self-image is the key ingredient in the recipe for success.

GOLDEN THOUGHTS TO DEPOSIT IN YOUR MIND BANK TO ACCUMULATE MORE INTEREST FOR YOU

1. The distance between success and failure is not measured by miles, but simply by one factor—the self-image.

2. While failures believe that successful people are lucky, successes know that personal efforts as a result of a positive, capable self-image are the reason for success.

3. Your self-image determines not only whether you will succeed or fail, your self-image determines whether you will be happy or unhappy, have ulcers, depression, hypertension, or live a satisfying physical life. Your self-image will even determine how long you will live. It is the single most important fact about you.

4. The great news is that your self-image can change and can change even if you have had a history of failure. Your self-image changes not simply by saying, "I'm a different person." Superficial attempts to fool your self-image are ineffective. Your self-image needs a systematic program to change. Self-image modification occurs when you develop the seven skills for success (Chapter III—Chapter IX).

5. Successes are those who are not only *ready* to take opportunities, but to *make* them as well.

CHAPTER II

Building Your Positive Self-Image to Become a Success Thinker

You can change—NOW. You can make your move towards success at this very moment. You can reach any dream that you have in mind by using the other 95% of your potential that you have left lying dormant. How? By building your positive self-image.

As you will soon see, when your self-image changes, everything in your life changes. Researchers have shown that students have gone from "F" grades to "A's" in a matter of weeks. Salespeople have literally doubled their income; shy people have become respected leaders; depressed people have developed a renewed enthusiasm for life. All of these changes have occurred because of one thing—a change in self-image.

Self-image is the ultimate determiner of personal success or failure. Your self-image is so important that one study after another concludes that your view of yourself is the key factor regulating your life. And the great news is that your self-image can change. Before getting you into the fun work of developing each of these seven building blocks of a positive self-image, immerse yourself in some of these interesting findings that researchers have discovered on the unparalleled power of your self-image.

In my search for the answer to the question, "Why do people fail?", I chanced upon a writer who could be considered the first advocate of the self-image psychology. In his insightful book, *Self Consistency: A Theory of Personality* (1945), the educator, Prescott Lecky, argued that people fail to succeed not because they are incapable of success, but because of their failure self-image. Lecky showed how negative preconceived beliefs and expectations build up resistances and convince people ahead of time that it would be impossible for them, with their limited capacities, to succeed. For example, if a person believes that learning a foreign language would be impossible, that person's self-image will fight to the bitter end to keep him or her from achieving success in speaking the new language. The second that the foreign language teacher enters the room, this convinced person resists the teacher's words.

To disprove the conclusion this person could not possibly learn the new language, note that even retarded people have learned foreign languages. But they only learn when they believe they can. If, however, their self-images resist, they will not learn. And, as a more humbling fact, even chimpanzees have learned to understand and respond to the English language! But chimps are lucky. Our hairy friends have an advantage over us. We spend all of our intelligence, reasoning power, and mental energies convincing ourselves that we cannot learn. We conclude that it would be too difficult to learn or perhaps too humiliating to try and maybe fail. If we used just half of that volcano of misdirected failure energy to actively tackle the task, we would succeed. So fear of failure as a result of a negative self-image is a sure guarantee of failure. With a positive self-image, however, the person envisions success and proceeds ahead to achieve that success.

EXPAND YOUR SELF-IMAGE, EXPAND YOUR POSSIBILITIES

Think about your own self-image. Have you ever limited your social possibilities by believing that there were certain men or women who were out of your social class? If you held these beliefs, what behavior would your failure beliefs dictate? You probably did not even approach these people to help get the relationship off the ground. Or, if you did approach them, perhaps you said some self-defeating things that sabotaged your chances of developing a relationship. Your self-image actually limited your pool of romantic possibilities. Imagine the number of romantic possibilities you would have just by expanding your self-image.

Did your self-image tell you that you deserve to live in a certain kind of house or that you deserve to have a certain level income? Did you listen to your self-image and buy that house or work to that exact level of income? And nothing more?

Evidence of the power of self-image is seen everywhere. For example, in the field of organizational development a common explanation used to demonstrate why promoted people sometimes fail is the well-known Peter Principle, developed by Dr. Lawrence Peter. People who are competent at one level are sometimes promoted to a higher level. The Peter Principle suggests that because the new level demands different skills, they often fail due to their lack of these new skills. The reason they fail, according to the Peter Principle, is because they were promoted to their level of incompetence.

I believe the Peter Principle is only partially correct. As a consultant to a few corporations, I found another reason to explain why some promoted people fail. If someone is promoted to a new position but his or her self-image views the position as too difficult or overwhelming, this person will fail. With expanding responsibilities must come expanded self-image. So people who are promoted, especially those who are promoted quickly, frequently need self-image expansion. Any organization wishing to tap the potential of its people needs to provide some sort of self-image expansion for its family members.

The owner of a major barber and beauty salon in Florida wanted to raise his prices for haircuts, but the barbers working for him resisted the price increase. His employees feared that a price raise would result in a loss of customers. I consulted with the owner, advising him that the barbers' resistance was not due to fear of losing customers, but rather their resistance was a result of their low self-image. They saw their styling abilities at too low a level. Their comment that they would lose customers was simply a comment on their self-image. They believed that they were not worth the new service charge. I advised the enthusiastic owner to help the barbers expand their self-images. This would help them to see their worth in new ways. I asked, "Have you asked your barbers how much they would pay, not for a hair style, but essentially for confidence, courage, and hope? Have you helped them see their profession, not their jobs, in a new light? If you do, and you help the barbers to develop a more positive and expanded self-image, they will beg you for the price increase. The price increase is your comment of respect for them. It shows that you believe in them."

As a college professor, I would often hear students make dogmatic comments such as, "I'm a B student," or "I'm an average student." I would always be tickled when one of these "B" students or "average students" would receive a great grade and share it almost apologetically with me. When I would proudly glance over the student's "A" grade, I would click my heels together and say, "Great job!" Strangely enough, with a self-image lower than the grade the student received, I'd hear something like, "Well, the only reason I received an A was because the professor was easy. I really should have earned a B, because I'm a B student."

Incredible, isn't it? Have you ever done the same? Why did the student need to apologize for the "A"?

WHY DO YOU INITIALLY REJECT NEW POSITIVE IDEAS ABOUT YOURSELF?

Prescott Lecky explained why the self-image always initially rejects a new view of itself. Lecky wrote, "The center of the nucleus of the mind is the individual's idea or conception of himself. If a new idea seems consistent with the ideas already present in the system, and particularly with the individual's conception of himself, it is accepted and assimilated easily. If it seems to be inconsistent, however, it meets with resistance and is likely to be rejected." (Lecky, 1945, p. 246.)

Lecky's theory of self-consistency was further supported by researchers who found that people's self-images of their abilities were better predictors of how they would achieve than were their I.Q.'s. Imagine that. It is not your ability but your beliefs about yourself that hold controlling interest in determining whether you will or will not succeed. Imagine the devastating cost of a negative self-image, because, in the end, if you believe you are incapable of success, your self-image will work overtime to make sure that success will not happen.

Other researchers, including W. B. Brookover and his associates, concluded from their studies that changes in a person's self-image lead to changes in achievement (1962). Again, this is powerful and exciting news. Your success is preceded by the belief that you can succeed. K. L. Harding, an educational researcher, showed that it could be predicted with reasonable certainty whether a student would or would not quit school just by knowing the student's self-image (1966).

In fact, a better gauge than any test devised of how a person will perform in a position is the person's self-image. On these astounding findings, the father of self-image research, William Purkey, writes in relation to school achievement and self-image:

> The conclusion seems unavoidable—a student carries with him certain attitudes about himself and his abilities which play the primary role in how he performs in school.

Lecky wondered why educators gave students remedial training when what the pupils really needed was an altered and positive vision that reflected the belief, "I can and will learn."

Did you ever see a person labelled "retarded" by one person in the presence of another person who believed in him or her? This person is like two different people in these different relationships. He or she performs much more successfully in the presence of the "believer." Consider yourself. Did you ever have a supervisor who didn't believe in you? Everything you did was viewed negatively. What happened? You probably began to feel incompetent. Conversely, did you ever have a supervisor who enthusiastically encouraged you to recognize your strengths and contributions? What happened? You performed—remember, the same you—probably more productively because of the person's beliefs and expectations!

Keep in mind that what you have just read is not opinion—it is scientifically researched fact. What you see is what you will be!

Concurring with Adler, Lecky, and others, Maxwell Maltz, the world-renowned plastic surgeon, wrote on this topic of self-image:

> The self-image is the key to human personality and human behavior. Change the self-image and you change the personality and behavior. But more than this. The self-image sets the boundaries of individual accomplishment. It defines what you can and cannot be. Expand the self-image and you expand the area of the possible. The development of an adequately realistic self-image will seem to imbue the individual with new capabilities, new talents, and literally turn failure into success. (Maltz, 1960, p. xix.)

It is perhaps no news to you that Maltz's book, *Psycho-Cybernetics,* is one of the best selling psychological classics of all time. Literally millions of people have been successfully influenced by this "self-determined psychology." Henry Ford's comment, "Believe you can or believe you can't—either way you'll be correct," is in tune with Maltz's and Lecky's and Adler's observations. In fact, Melvin Powers, the publisher of this book and the paperback publisher of *Psycho-Cybernetics,* upon reading the book for the first time, predicted that *Psycho-Cybernetics* would sell millions of copies. And it did! Powers didn't have that positive success insight by looking into a crystal ball. No, Melvin Powers concluded ahead of time that the book without a doubt was going to be a winner. And he proceeded to make it happen. He looked to the skies and set his goals high!

Just how do these powerful ideas of self-image psychology work to create success?

HOW DOES THE SELF-IMAGE PRODUCE SUCCESS OR FAILURE?

"I could never speak in front of a group."

"I'm not built to be a leader."

"I'm the kind of person who has difficulty making decisions."

"Me! I'd never make it in sales. Selling requires something I don't have."

"I'm afraid to try new things or take risks."

"Quit smoking? Not me! I just lack self-discipline."

"No, I'd never ask her out. She'd never want anything to do with me."

"I have average intelligence."

"I'm a $20,000-a-year person."

"I'm the kind of person who is shy."

"I just can't resist snacks."

"I'm not good at opening up new sales accounts."

"I can't take any pressure on the job. I get migraines when given too much responsibility."

"I'm a C student."

"I've gone about as far as I can go."

Have you ever heard any of these statements? Please note a few things that each of these statements has in common:

1. Each statement is an echo of the individual's self-image, e.g., "I'm the kind of person who is shy" is a comment on the way this person views him or herself.
2. Each self-image statement is inaccurate, i.e., it can be disproven. As you glance over the list, look closely at each comment, and you will see that each conclusion could be challenged.
3. Although each self-image statement is inaccurate, the speaker is not consciously aware that the comment is inaccurate and proceeds through life as if the pronouncement were carved in his or her behavioral granite. The opinion of self is treated by the person as if it were a fact.
4. Each self-image statement limits the individual's potential success. As long as the person believes this conclusion to be a fact, for that exact period of time no growth in this area can occur.
5. When the individual's subconscious recognizes that the statement is an inaccurate observation which he or she has treated as if it were a fact, he or she can then attack the false conclusion and proceed to expand the self-

defeating self-image to one of success. This process is called self-image modification and is the theme of this book.

Observe how a person's negative self-image prevents that individual from achieving success. Consider the statement, "I could never speak in front of groups." This comment is a reflection of the speaker's self-image. The speaker feels that this is an absolute fact about himself or herself. Ask yourself, "What are facts and what are opinions?" Two plus two equals four is a fact. Is "I could never speak in front of groups" a fact or an opinion? Yes, it is the person's opinion. Yet the self-image does not know this and treats the opinion as if it were a fact. When this happens, the person experiences anxieties and fears about public speaking. These emotional arousals force this person to avoid any situation or opportunity to overcome the "can't." The self-image guides the person away from any incident where he or she may be asked to do anything that resembles public speaking. Consequently, the person will never have the experience to achieve success. For the rest of the individual's life, this opinion, treated as fact, will prevent him from achieving success as a public speaker. He needs a change in self-image before success can happen.

The "I could never" statements are self-defeating. Probably as a toddler the first time you tried to take a step, you fell flat on your face. Suppose that you then concluded (pre-verbally, of course) that because you fell over, "you could never" walk like Mommy and Daddy. If you concluded that, you would never try to walk again. After all, you tried to walk one time and you fell flat on your face, so you "could never" walk. Imagine the embarrassment you would experience today, arriving at a cocktail party. You would crawl into the room and pull the tablecloth down to reach for the hors d'oeuvres.

You succeeded because, when you fell, your self-image kept envisioning yourself as a person who could, or who soon would, walk, and fortunately you followed your self-image that said you could walk, with practice. And you did.

Remember the first time you tried to drive a car? You were probably tense, and perhaps your jumpiness caused you to panic and quickly slam on the brakes. Maybe your anxious reaction almost put you and your parents through the front windshield. The earth-shattering experience could have even led you to break down in tears, proclaiming dogmatically, "I can never learn how to do something as tough as driving a car!" Maybe you even put yourself down because you believed the same task of driving appeared to be so easy for everyone else. A negative self-image steered you away from trying again. Then something happened. At some point your self-image saw hope and "envisioned" success. Your new capable self-image may have concluded, "It will be tough to drive, but I will eventually learn how." Maybe you had a few more negative experiences while practicing, but each moment you improved and you soon succeeded. Now, today, with the self-image, "I am capable," you jump into the car, turn on the ignition, turn on the radio, depress the clutch, and one-handedly drive for hundreds of miles as you glance at the billboards and scenic mountainsides without a single nervous thought. You achieved success simply as a result of a positive self-image that predicted success. Your positive self-image overcame a few failing incidents by a positive hopeful vision. And you want to make your actions fit your vision of yourself as a successful driver.

Now reconsider our friend who proclaims, "I could never speak in front of a group." This person is no different than the young child who "could never walk" or the teenager who "could never drive." The individual is a diamond with a rough negative self-image. The culprit denying success for this potential Demosthenes is not the lack of public speaking ability, poor vocabulary, or even fear of groups. The only criminal is the negative self-image that shouts, "I could never!" Think of it! Imagine that this person's self-image concluded, "It will be tough, but with work I could speak in front of groups." What a monumental move to success for the person. Now the blossoming person will develop a new plan of action to overcome those limited visions. A capable and positive self-image is the key ingredient to start the success snowball rolling.

FROM A FEAR OF PUBLIC SPEAKING TO A CAREER IN LECTURING THROUGH SELF-IMAGE MODIFICATION

I choose the example of public speaking because it touches home with me. I would like to share with you a personal story.

A decade before the completion of this manuscript, I went to hear a lecture. While watching the dynamic speaker, I became inspired that what he did was what I was going to someday do. I wanted to be the best speaker I could possibly be in my one lifetime. However, I wasn't talented in speaking. In fact, my vocabulary and grammar scores on achievement tests were in the bottom 10% of my high school class. I was frightened to death about even the thought of speaking in front of crowds of people. So I had a lot—a whole lot—to overcome. However, the only resistance I had to overcome was in my mind. But I visualized success and I wanted it. I knew that there was absolutely NO WAY that I wouldn't reach my goal during my lifetime.

Because I visualized my goal and became determined, my course was locked in. My compass was pointed towards a goal. My self-image believed that "with much work, it could be accomplished." So I developed my plan. My ears and eyes were open to sense opportunities to observe good speakers. I travelled distances just to watch speakers' professional mannerisms. Keep in mind that I would have never done this if my self-image had concluded ahead of time that my goal was unattainable.

I started my first lectures by talking to chairs in my living room, imagining these chairs were people. I looked into a mirror while I spoke and developed expressive looks and hand gestures. I followed this by taking every opportunity I had to speak to small groups. I worked diligently to improve my poor vocabulary and grammar. I literally did everything consistent with my goal for success. I had many setbacks, observed people walking out during my talks, bored to death. But I remembered my goal, keeping in mind that these experiences were all a necessary part of achieving my destination. I personally experienced shaking knees, white knuckles, and chattering teeth many times, but the "success force" in me kept pushing me onward towards my goal.

As I think of it, the destination was inevitable since I visualized my goal and concluded that there was NO WAY I couldn't reach it. When discouraged, my self-image kept envisioning a sign on the highway of life which read:

NEXT EXIT—NOWHERE
STRAIGHT AHEAD—EVERYWHERE

I'm still on that road following my compass that points toward success. Today, I make my living through lecturing to hundreds of thousands of people annually. Every time I told myself, "I could never speak in public," I was wrong. I always could; I just needed a self-image that concluded ahead of time that the day would come when I would achieve my goal. Once I prophesied success, I developed my plan and moved towards the goal. If I made a mistake, I simply corrected the problem. The next time I moved closer to my goal.

On this highway of life, successful achievement of your goals is like driving your car from New York to Los Angeles. When you start, you are at the farthest point from your goal. You cannot possibly be at your goal at that minute of starting, but you can keep focusing on the fact that you are moving towards your goal. If you keep your goal firmly locked in mind when your car fails, you will quickly get it fixed. Complaining about the disabled car only wastes your valuable success time and delays your victory celebration day.

THE SELF-IMAGE PROPHESIES SUCCESS OR FAILURE

David's job interview is only a few minutes away. As the 20-year-old lad waits tensely outside the personnel manager's office, he thinks about how unsuccessful he has been in previous interviews. Reflecting on the last four jobs that he didn't get, he thinks, "Why should this one be any different?" In addition to being on a job-seeking losing streak, he reminds himself about all of the news on how tight the job market is. He is certain that there are probably many people much more qualified for this job than he. Although his background fits the requirements on paper, he thinks there surely will be someone else who has either more experience, more education, or more of an "in." He slumps in his chair as he looks around the room crowded with competition for the same position. And he is sure that every one of them has something that he lacks. To escape eye-to-eye contact with his competitors, he glances at the secretary. She appears to be meticulously organized and aloof. She peers at David over the top of her glasses with intimidating looks. David squirms again. His heart is pounding, his voice seems to be leaving, his palms are sweating, his chin is quivering, and his knees are shaking. He wants to leave and, at that moment, the personnel manager opens the door and announces, "David, come into my office."

Jonathan's job interview is only a few minutes away. The 20-year-old man waits outside the personnel manager's office with eager anticipation. He begins to think about how he can be a success on the job once he gets the position. He analyzes the position he is seeking and mentally lives a day in the life of a person in that capacity. It is a position in which he would be dealing with people, and he loves people. Jonathan imagines that he owns the company. He wonders what kind of a person he would want in that position for his company. What kind of attitudes would he be looking for in the people that he would hire? He concludes that he would want a person who likes people, who is confident, who is open to new ideas, who is enthusiastic, and who would be a good company employee. Yes, Jonathan thinks, to be a good company employee, it would be wise to learn more about the company. He looks around the reception area and finds a company brochure on the table. He pages through the brochure and becomes excited about the company. He learns some interesting facts about the size and scope of the operation. This news excites him and tells him of his opportunities to grow. Jonathan looks at the office and imagines himself with an office of his own. The secretary, obviously efficient, stares over her glasses at him, and Jonathan gives her a big ear-to-ear smile. She smiles back. Jonathan feels good inside and thinks how warm the people are in this company. He is also impressed with her efficiency and kindly shares with her his observation. Impressed, he comments, "I really admire your organization. Are you one of those naturally organized people?" The secretary replies, "I guess I enjoy my work." She smiles again. He already feels he belongs there . . . and he does . . . and he soon will be.

David and Jonathan are stories of life. David's negative self-image dictated to his whole viscera the notion that he doesn't deserve the position and that he will never get it. As a result, David's self-image worked vigorously to defeat him. The personnel manager, in reading David's confidence level, saw him as a person who would be too timid, too defensive, to be a part of a growing assertive company. David does not get the position and he is defeated again. For the next job interview, his self-image will be even more negative. The lad's self-image predicted failure and the prediction became accurate.

Jonathan, on the converse, carries a self-image that announces the arrival of success. Jonathan predicted success for himself and thus used his energies to make that success happen. While David squirmed in his seat, Jonathan went ahead and learned more about the company, imagined what kind of employee the company needed in that position, and, in fact, ignited his own enthusiasm for the job.

The same situation was faced by David and Jonathan. Yet observe how different it looked to each because of the different self-image eyeglasses that each wore. David saw obstacles, and Jonathan saw opportunity. When you have a self-image that asserts, "I can and will succeed," the world looks different, more promising, and exciting. Even the secretary appeared different to both.

If you were the personnel manager, which person would you hire for your sales or management position?

Both David and Jonathan had predictions about the results of the interview. Both prophecies were accurate. David believed he couldn't get the job and he was accurate; Jonathan believed he could be successful in earning the position and he was accurate, too.

Baruch Spinoza, the philosopher, concluded that, "As long as a person believes that a certain task is impossible, for the exact period of time the task will be." Everything that you believe you can't do is totally 100% accurate—until you turn the corner and start to tackle each "can't" slowly and constructively. It is my estimate that 75 to 90% of a person's "can'ts" are really "won'ts," not "can'ts."

Your self-image produces success or failure by prophesying or subconsciously predicting success or failure. The most important quality of your self-image is that it is a prophet. As a prophet, it is constantly gazing into an almost infallible crystal ball predicting your future.

SELF-IMAGE . . . PROPHECY OF FUTURE

Consider a salesperson whose self-image concludes, "I'm the kind of person who can't open up new accounts." This person's conclusion is wrong. The self-image acts "as if" the conclusion were accurate. This person's self-image is narrow and naive. Yet, it matters not that the conclusion is wrong as long as the self-image believes it is accurate.

Imagine that this salesperson who draws the conclusion, "I'm the kind of person who can't open up new accounts," is called in by the sales manager. The sales manager asserts, "It's about time you open up some new accounts for our company. Let's see you start knocking on some new doors tomorrow." Can you feel this person's anxieties about the next day? With this person's self-image of "I'm the kind of person who can't open up new accounts," what prophecy or expectation is made about tomorrow's possibilities?

Self-Image	Prophecy, expectations, prediction
"I'm the kind of person who can't open up new accounts."	"I'll go out, but I know I'll never succeed." The person knocks on doors and apologizes, or out of anxiety becomes pushy and loses sales.

The salesman's negative self-image prophesied failure and subconsciously controlled his or her behavior to make the failure happen. What would it be worth for the salesperson and the employer to develop this person's self-image to make it one like Jonathan's—one filled with success? I believe almost anything! That is the goal of this book—developing your positive self-image through the seven ingredients that successful people with positive self-images have.

How do you develop your positive self-image? Your self-image is made positive not by just saying, "I'm confident." That would be phony and superficial, and your self-image would read right through the facade.

Your positive self-image is developed through a systematic process. Chapters III to IX are an intensive self-image development program. Please do not read more than one chapter at a sitting. It will just be too overwhelming. Make each chapter of this book a part of your life. Chapter X, Taking Up Permanent Residence on the Street of Success, provides a checklist to keep your positive self-image on the course to a happy, successful, and productive life. For an effective personal success program that lasts, specific guidelines are given in Chapter X.

DEVELOP YOUR POSITIVE SELF-IMAGE

A positive self-image is one that "automatically" thinks success and steers you on to achieving your goals and becoming the person you want to be. How do you build your positive self-image? By developing each of the seven skills and attitudes that comprise a positive self-image.

The seven factors that guarantee you a positive self-image are:

1. creative thinking
2. enthusiasm
3. goal-centering
4. environmental designing
5. rational thinking
6. leadership
7. getting started

"GIVE YOUR SELF-IMAGE A RAISE" WITH THESE REMINDERS

1. 75 to 90% of those goals you believe you can't achieve, you can. Compose a list of ten items that you believe you can't achieve. Now, thinking carefully and successfully, cross out every item that was not really a "can't" but was, in fact, a "won't." Get Off Your "Can'ts!" Think CAN. Success comes in CANS!

2. When you expand your self-image, you expand your possibilities. Think small, be small; think tall, be tall!

3. Your self-image is a prophet for your future. Like David, your self-image may be prophesying failure. Or like Jonathan, your self-image may be prophesying success.

4. Underestimate yourself or overestimate yourself. Either way, you will work vigorously to make your estimate accurate.

5. The scientific facts are in: success, happiness, and achievement often occur even before your actions. They can be predicted by what

your self-image imagines will happen. Give your self-image a raise and success, happiness, and achievement are yours.

Open up your mind and fire up your will. A whole new refreshing, enriching life will soon be yours. It's time to begin your journey to Success City by an intensive self-image development program.

Now to the first building block of success, creative thinking. In the next few hours, you will be worth more to yourself just by learning how to unleash your creative potential.

CHAPTER III

Achieving Success By Unleashing Your Creative Potential

Can you remember times in your childhood when you helped your family plan the rearrangement of your living room furniture? Can you recall the excitement you experienced just by thinking about how the new room would look? You tried different ideas—some had it, some didn't. And then, the moment arrived. The winning combination was put together and it felt like an entirely new room. You experienced a refreshing feeling as you plopped yourself down on the same old "new" couch for the first time!

Your creative rearrangement of the furniture had the power to revitalize your spirits. You were invigorated by experiencing things in a new way. A whole new living room was yours through the life-giving powers of creative thinking. And what is creative thinking? Nothing more than a rearrangement of your mental furniture. The beauty of creative thinking is that it doesn't cost you a penny. Creative thinking is free.

SUCCESS IS A GOOD IDEA

The Skyscraper of Success is constructed from only one kind of material—IDEAS. Yes, the ability to develop new ideas is why the human being reigns over the earth. Civilization has progressed from the cave to the country club because of ... IDEAS. Some diseases that have

45

plagued humankind for centuries are now extinct because of . . . IDEAS. Depressions, fears, and anxieties are being conquered today, once again because of . . . IDEAS. (For further detail on coping with your negative emotions, see Chapter VII, Rational Thinking.)

All progress, all success, flows from the IDEAS of creative, courageous people. Creative people succeed because they are willing to use their thinking powers to look at the world in new ways. Courageous people become successful because they dare to break from the security of the old and reach to find the treasures of the unknown. So, when you are both a creative and courageous person, you experience a panoramic view of life with its unlimited number of ideas.

HOW MANY IDEAS ARE IN THE WORLD?

How many ideas are there in the world? Well, how high is up? How many colors are there in the world? How wide is the universe? The world is a vast library, your library, extending to the sun and beyond, to the very edges of the universe, and it is filled with trillions of thoughts and ideas accumulated over a billion years of history.

Feel free to select ideas from this infinite source of knowledge and be creative with them. Remember, it is your library. Use your will to unlock the annals of time so that you can experience and share the thoughts and ideas of the past, understand the reasons for the present, and form the basis of your future. You have a lifelong membership in this library, and you may draw as many ideas from it as you wish for as long as you like. How many ideas are there in the world? The number is infinite.

The philosopher Bertrand Russell commented, "In the vast realm of the alive human mind, there are no limitations." The fact that you have this unlimited potential in a world with unlimited ideas proves that you were originally designed for success. And successfully achieving your goals is as natural as the growth of the tiny seedling into the giant oak.

CASH IN ON THE IDEAS ALREADY PRESENT IN YOUR MIND BANK

Each and every day of your life is a payday. And each day of your life, you subconsciously deposit an unlimited number of ideas into your Mind Bank. Yet, very rarely do you allow yourself to cash in on any of your rich deposits. Unfortunately, the Mind Bank doesn't pay interest to you unless you pay interest to it.

Get your withdrawal slip ready. You are about to fill up your pockets from a vault full of ideas by becoming a creative thinker. Now ... step confidently and enthusiastically into your Mind Bank to claim and monopolize on the riches of your own ideas.

EXTRACTING THE GOLD FROM YOUR MIND THROUGH THE TEN STEPS TO CREATIVITY

Step 1.   C—Challenge yourself to change.
Step 2.   R—Relax and daydream of the possible.
Step 3.   E—Experience a constant, fresh view of life.
Step 4.   A—Assume that every problem has a solution.
Step 5.   T—Trust your own ideas.
Step 6.   I —Invite the ideas of others.
Step 7.   V—Visualize success.
Step 8.   I —Ink your contract with yourself.
Step 9.   T—Take positive action on your ideas.
Step 10.   Y—Yield to even newer ideas.

Step 1. C—Challenge Yourself to Change

Rearrange your mental furniture. Change is as good as a break. It can restore youthfulness regardless of your chronological age. Absorb new and different ideas. Say "Sayonara" to that part of you that feels stagnated. Give yourself that "new bedsheet feeling" by looking at yourself and your world in new, refreshing ways.

Can ideas change? You "betcher" gold tooth on it! Can you remember times when a new insight gained entry into your mind and heart and, like electricity, sparked new life? I can. I recall one incident quite vividly when I realized I had the power to change my ideas on a moment's notice. It happened one bright March afternoon in the Chinatown section of San Francisco. Following lunch in a colorful pagoda-type rice shop, ages of Eastern wisdom appeared to me in my fortune cookie. The seed of inspirational thought in my dessert read, "THERE IS STILL YET TIME ENOUGH FOR YOU TO CHANGE YOUR COURSE OF ACTION IN LIFE."

The powerful yet simple insight hit me—as long as there is life, there is time to change that life. Within a few moments, I had made a decision that literally affected my whole future. I headed my life in an entirely new professional direction—a direction that I had wanted for a long time, but thought that it was too late to change. What about you? Are you ready to place a bet on your possibilities? Dare yourself to change!

1. *Trade in your old self-image for a new one.* Brush the cobwebs, the barnacles, and the dust off of your old ways of looking at yourself. Get out of the "This is the kind of person I am" rut. Shed some light on your inexhaustible potential. Create some new ways of looking at yourself. Build a new self-image that is broader, richer, and fresher. Make a commitment to the belief that anything is possible for the new you!

2. *Change yourself by following the model of your mother—Mother Nature!* For example, look at the seasons of the year and how they change by flowing naturally from one to the other. Think of the refreshing beauty each "new" season gives us. Experience the trees in their four different wardrobes (if you happen to live in a climate that will allow that possibility). Watch the thinly-clad maple of winter dress piece by piece into its fine green outfit of spring and reach full maturity in the summer. And especially observe the new growth each year. Mother Nature has not only designed change into her cyclical arrangements, she has also cleverly provided for constant and progressive growth. Like the maple "goldens" with the fall telling of its plan to undress the old ideas during the winter and appear again in a few months fresh and green, so the human "silvers" with the wisdom which comes from a similar reevaluation, change and growth. Yes, change is natural, beautiful, and moving.

Experience the beauty of nature's movement by observing the power of a flowing river. Hiking through the mountains of Banff, Alberta, I had the opportunity to contrast two types of bodies of water. First, I watched with amazement a swiftly flowing effervescent stream doing a fast dance through the Canadian Rockies. In its movement, the water was literally autographing the basin and the mountains. What an impact the movement created! The water was clear, fresh, cool, and exciting to watch. Why not, since it was unpredictable. It was changing every second.

Only a few hundred yards away, I chanced upon a stagnant pond. It was lifeless and boring. The water was dark and brackish. Its best claim was that it could invite a yawn on the face of the rare observer. It was predictable and offered the same motionless picture today as it had done yesterday, and the day before. Have you ever met people who were like the same motionless, predictable, stagnant pond? Not yourself! Start now. Be determined that you will be more like the exciting, changing flowing river. Challenge yourself to feature a new motion picture of ideas every day.

3. *Change by observing people who are growing and changing.* Watch the styles of people you know who are interesting to be with. Do they not amaze you with their ceaseless energy to look at old things in

new ways? Do they not associate with many different people, thereby getting a variety of ideas? Interesting people literally work and have fun at being interesting. They have a zest for life. They provide hope in tough situations. They say hello first, rather than waiting for someone else to start the conversation. They sit up front in church or at a lecture. They are where the action is. They are on the go. They act in life rather than complain about it. Yes, pick out a few of the most interesting people you know and find the lively patterns that you see in them. Be willing to change your ideas by listening to the ideas of the most interesting people you know. Listen to "pick-up" people.

4. *Challenge yourself to change your ideas.* Dare to question your old ideas, even those beliefs that you have held for a time. Challenge yourself to have the openness to the new. A new baby gives life to the people nearby. So do new ideas. Read books that advocate the opposite position that you hold on an issue. They will stimulate you. Your ideas, if valid, will hold up, and even become stronger with a closer, more rigorous inspection. But if you find that your beliefs are crumbling, they are not worthy of you anyway. Challenge yourself to change by courageously inspecting your current ideas and beliefs.

5. *Challenge stale thinkers who say that new things can't be done.* Rise above the belief that the way things are now is the only way they can be. How depressing a belief! Imagine if every person in the world concluded that things can't get any better. What would happen? Every medical researcher looking for cures for cancer, heart attacks, or any other diseases would change professions. Every medical research lab in the world would close its doors. Every scientist looking for solutions to the world's energy crisis would conclude that there are no answers. The world would use up all of its resources and humankind would slowly regress. Every parent who has a young child with behavioral or emotional problems would reason that there is no hope, the child will never change.

Don't get caught in the "things can't change" claptrap. You know that there are cures for the different types of cancer. You know that answers will be found to deal with the energy problems of the world, and you know that the problem child can and will change. But any of these changes can take place only when people have the courage to look at things in new ways. No new look, no change. Believe that things can't change, and you're right—they can't.

In conclusion, the first step in developing your powers of creative thinking is to challenge yourself to change your ideas. You do this by (1) trading in your self-image for a new, more refreshing one, (2) following the changes that you see in nature, (3) observing people who are growing and changing, (4) challenging your old ideas and letting in new ones, and (5) confronting stale thinkers who believe that things can't change.

The second step in developing your powers of creative thinking is to get rid of that part of you that resists new ideas. You can do this by relaxing and daydreaming of the possible.

Step 2. R—Relax and Daydream of the Possible

After challenging your old ideas, the next step to becoming more creative is to stop blocking new ideas. That part of you that resists new ideas can be eliminated in a few minutes by simply relaxing and turning down the noise in your mind. Find the most comfortable chair available or lie on the bed or floor if you like. If you choose, you may have someone you trust read the following imagining exercise to you very slowly. If not, read a paragraph at a time for yourself and take a little time to immerse yourself in the experience. Then move on to the next paragraph and do likewise. Let yourself go. Ready?

Imagination Exercise to Eliminate the
Idea-Blocking Forces and to Unleash
Your Powers of Creativity

As you find yourself relaxed, say, "At this minute there is absolutely no pressure at all on me." None. Now feel a sense of freshness. At this moment, I would like to share some great news with you. In the next few minutes, it is possible to eliminate every part of you that blocks your creativity. These negative parts of you keep you from creating newer, more refreshing ideas that will be the source of a more positive self-image for you.

To do so, I invite you to come with me to my special place where we can dump our excess negative baggage. Come with me to my home on Long Beach Island, a little island off the coast of New Jersey. For the next few minutes, we will be overlooking the magnificent Atlantic Ocean, a garden of water flowering in foam. It matters not whether you are living in poverty or are a millionaire, whether you are on your first or last breath, or whether you are six or one-hundred-and-six years of age. The only requirement to a newer self-image is a willingness to relax. If you are ready to turn down the noise in your mind, let's go to the bubbling ocean.

It's five o'clock in the morning as we walk over the dunes protected by a wooden picket fence and catch our first glimpse of our never-tiring friend, the breathtaking Atlantic. (Pause.) It is still dark here on the beach except for the full moon's last smiles of the night on the dancing ocean and, of course, the psychedelic spotlights of the smooth breaking waves. (Pause.)

We walk closer to the ocean and find a comfortable spot to stand on the beach. Our feet are occasionally being tickled by the final comments of a smooth breaking wave undertowing its way towards a new destiny. Feel your toes being urged to surrender themselves to the wet, white beach sand. (Pause.) Experience the warm, whistling breeze on your back trying to nudge you into the sea. (Pause.) Watch the cowardly sandpipers challenge the saltwater and run away when the huge ocean accepts their challenge. (Pause.) Feel the restful scene for a few moments by adding any additional experiences you could sense in the early morning setting. Let your imagination flow. (Pause until fully immersed in the setting.)

It's time to continue. I hand to you a huge empty beach bag. I ask you to open the bag to prepare for removing all of your negative nonsense, your excess baggage, forever. First, I encourage you to put into your bag every ounce of fear that you have. At the top of your list of fears is your fear of making a mistake, the biggest culprit to your progress. A whole new life is available to you the moment you rid yourself of the fear of making mistakes. While ninety-nine percent of the people in the world who fail, fail because of the fear of trying something new, you will be the mountain climber, the leader, because of your courage to overcome this fear and to "do." You are fully aware that your willingness to explore new horizons will at times result in mistakes. But the solution to true success is simple: when you fall, you will simply pick yourself up. (Pause.) With the warm, soft breeze at your back, take a few seconds, relax, and commit yourself to throwing your fear of making mistakes into your bag of negative nonsense forever. (Pause until ready to go on.)

Next, while watching the first seagull of the morning gracefully soar and descend in hopeful search of an early morning breakfast, I encourage you to add to your new sense of courage by throwing into your bag every part of you that still lives in the past. Focusing on past romances, past failures, past mistakes, even past successes is a retreat from life's potential adventure today. Living in the ideas of a past that could literally never return is a sure guarantee that you will not see what is possible today or tomorrow. Looking to your past is like running backwards in your race to success. Even if your past has been the worst of anyone's in the world, with lack of love, rejection, bitterness, and discouragement, the great news is that the past is past. Today, if you choose, a whole new life is available for you. While rubbing bodies with your loyal friend, the enthusiastic ocean, become determined to throw that part of you that lives in the past into your bag of negative nonsense. While doing so, say to yourself meaningfully, five times, the words, "My past is past and hooray for today!" (Pause until ready to go on.)

Now, while listening to the ocean clapping, with the beach cheering your new life on, I urge you to put into your bag of nonsense all of the blame that you still have within you. Blame is at the root of all personal stagnation. Blame produces all negative emotions that sap your success energies. Include in your bag of nonsense all blame, even of people who make you angry, like your parents, your bosses, or your enemies. People living on Angry Avenue can't succeed and they are unpleasant to be near. Your one fleeting moment in the history of our universe is too important to be used handcuffed by anger and revenge. By making a commitment now to forgive and forget others, you can be assured of having a clean slate of fresh new energies to create new ideas. And if you are religious, you can feel in harmony with the Almighty by forgiving and forgetting as God does when you ask to have your mistakes forgiven and forgotten. (Brief pause.)

Along with the blame of others, throw into your bag the part of you that blames yourself. Guilt is unproductive. Instead of feeling guilty or ashamed of yourself, feel determined to change. If you are going to do good for the world, you need to be inspired by a desire to help, not motivated by a sense of guilt. Relax, feel the playful surf tickling your toes, and throw all blame of yourself, others, and the world into your bag of negative nonsense forever. When you stop blaming, you start living! (Pause until ready to move on.)

Finally, while standing on the wet, white, sandy beach, freshly cleaned by the overnight washing of the high tide, put into your bag everything that you feel ashamed, apologetic, or defensive about. This includes every reason you still use for not allowing yourself to become a reinvigorated person with new ideas. As you know, failures are quite talented at apologizing, defending, and excusing. In fact, the bigger the failure, the more talented he or she is at making excuses. In the future, when you have an impulse to defend youself, force yourself to stop defending and to start changing. So, like successes do, throw into your bag of negatives, all apologies, excuses, and defenses. Take charge, rise above loser thinking, and march through life proudly for who you are, regardless of what anyone else thinks. You are a human being who has as much right to exist as anyone, and you need not explain or justify your new ideas to anybody. Relax, take a few seconds, and become determined that you will live your life in a creative and non-defensive way. Proudly throw in that part of you that previously apologized, excused, and defended your life. (Pause for as long as necessary.)

You have now relaxed by the seashore and have removed from your system your fear of making a mistake; your practice of living in the past; your habit of blaming other people, yourself and life; and finally, your need to apologize, defend, or excuse yourself. Your toes are firmly immersed in the Long Beach Island sand, the warm island breeze is at your back, the lights of a few fishing boats are decorating the horizon, and the powerful Atlantic Ocean is brewing a spicy effervescence for you. Now imagine there is a piece of string lying conveniently on the beach near you. Take the string and tightly close the top of your bag with it. Look around you now. There is also a huge yellow and blue kite lying near you. It is a very powerful kite and can lift anything with the ease of a seagull. Pick up the kite and firmly tie your bag of negatives to it. (Pause.)

On the count of three, let your kite go and ascend naturally into the strong Atlantic Ocean wind in its destination to Never Again Land. (Pause.) The breeze picks up as the count begins. One, . . . look ahead with excitement and anticipation to a new, refreshed life. (Pause.) Two, . . . your fingers prepare themselves to free you for a positive new life. (Pause.) Three, . . . let go of your fears, your past, your blame, and your apologies for living. You can watch your kite drift away from you towards Never Again Land. The breeze is strong, and the kite gets smaller and smaller. Soon you can no longer see the negative at all. You are now a refreshed and creative new person with all of your energies geared toward success. All of a sudden, you can see the sun peering over the horizon, tipping its golden hat in a friendly gesture of hello. The sun brings good news, announcing the arrival of spring in your life. (Pause.)

Anything is possible for you because you can create without fear. Any new idea can gracefully flow through your system without being immediately judged or condemned. With your fresh new life, you have expanded the area of the possible.

It is now time to dream of the possible through the use of positive thinking.

Positive Thinkers Have the Midas Touch
by Daydreaming of the Possible

Your life is now freed of a tremendous negative burden. Watch how you have the power to increase the value of any part of your life. You can enrich your life simply by applying your mental Midas touch. Allow me to get you started by providing an example of how the Midas touch works. Let us take a common, everyday pencil. A negative thinker, always afraid to make a mistake and always viewing things in terms of the precedents of the past, can only see a pencil as being "something to write with." But you, a positive and creative thinker, can literally, yes, literally, increase the value of this pencil in only one minute. Without the fear of making a mistake and by using your Midas touch, you can expand the pencil's worth. Let's daydream of the pencil's possibilities. The pencil could be used to teach a child a certain color; for example, "this is a *yellow* pencil." That same pencil could be used to protect yourself if attacked. How much would that be worth? The pencil could be used to bite on when tense or to write up a sales order. It could even be employed as a putter if you don't have one on the golf course. Perhaps not as effective as a real putter, but it still could be. In fact, that pencil, the one in your mind right now, could be used to change the course of human history!

Now, in just a few seconds, that single pencil has increased in value because of an open mind. See the power in the ability to use creative thinking? And just imagine—if in *one minute's time* you can increase the value of a pencil just by looking at it in new ways, think what you could do with everything else around you over a 30,000-day lifetime! And even more amazing is the fact that there are no limits to the amount of uses the pencil, or anything, has. If only you are courageous, live in the present, and don't block the possibilities.

And, as a final booster, if in one minute's time we could create six new possibilities for a pencil, imagine what possibilities exist for yourself—a living, breathing human being—over the course of a whole lifetime? What you could be is what you really are. It's just waiting for your willingness to see the possible. You have the Midas touch.

In this step, you have challenged yourself to change by looking at things and yourself in new ways. Next, you relaxed, eliminated the negative blocking forces within you, and daydreamed of the possible. Now add to your creative thinking power by experiencing a fresh view of life.

Step 3. E—Experience a Constant Fresh View of Life

My friend Dennis Boike, a Rochester, New York, psychologist, tells me, "Wherever you are, be there." Well, it's easy to "be there" when you are the guest of a frothing ocean or a majestic mountain. But the really creative person can be inspired not only by the flawless symmetry of a flower, but also by sensually rearranging the familiar. Open your eyes. your ears, your mouth, nose and hands to let fresh experiences flow in, to rearrange your mental furniture.

1. *Experience a constant fresh view of life by getting more "awake" time in your day.* Enthuse yourself with the idea of getting up a few minutes earlier than you currently do. You can do this by planning in excited anticipation of the new day before going to bed. Never go to sleep without developing a positive plan for yourself for the next day. Always make the next day be the special day that you have been waiting for. Every day can be your "Birth of New Ideas Day"! What do you enjoy doing? Is it a walk through some rustling leaves, a morning cup of tea in your courtyard, or listening to your favorite music? In your extra "awake" time, could you prepare a special breakfast to break the monotony of mornings in your household? Or would a nice warm bath while reading from the works of your favorite author, rather than the usual shower, suit your fancy? Your goal for the day need not be elaborate. Make the ordinary the extraordinary. "Hit the spot." Plan for what makes you happy and awaken earlier with a positive new vitality and a positive view of life.

2. *Experience a constant fresh view of life by reminding yourself a few times each day that you are alive.* Make it a point to feel the cool springs of your existence by recognizing all of your alternatives. When you forget your alternatives, you put yourself on automatic pilot, like a robot. And, as all automatons, robots do not think for themselves or keep themselves in a state of repair. You must maintain your spirit and stay awake and alive, directing your own destiny. Do the unusual. Drive yourself to work or school a different way. You even have alternatives other than your car. Take the bicycle out of the garage and "bike it" to work. Experience a constant fresh view of life by being in touch with the fact that you are alive, and this in itself gives you many, many alternatives.

3. *Experience a constant fresh view of people by looking for the positive in everyone you know.* Find something novel and interesting in everyone. Be a talent scout. Talent scouts can see beyond the surface and can visualize the hidden resources and assets in people. When you become a talent scout and constantly experience new ways of looking at people, you will find something interesting happens. Your popularity will soar like a thermometer on the equator.

4. *Experience a constant fresh view of people as well by staying away from stale conversations that focus on small talk.* Make it unfashionable for people to be petty thinkers around you. Be the first one to reroute a "talk-behind-someone's-back" conversation by pointing out the assets of the defenseless person. You will soon find that everyone will trust you more. (If you don't talk about other people, they assume logically you won't talk about them either.) You are a source of less hurting and a source of more confidence.

5. *Experience a constant fresh view of life by taking those things that life gives you and combine them in original ways.* For example, if you enjoy cooking, consider what the great chefs of the world do. They take the same foods that are available to everyone and combine them in new, unique, tasteful recipes. They constantly experiment by using some elements of the old when creating the new. Instead of serving the usual salad today, add something new to make it special. A complete new salad dish personally autographed by you.

How many soups are there in the world? There are as many as you choose to create. My Canadian friend and chef, Vi Love, makes a constant practice of combining different fruits and vegetables into new arrangements. What a thrill to smell and taste a carrot-orange or a cream of avocado soup for the first time.

How many songs are there in the world? Again, the number is up to you. While the same basic notes are available to everyone, creative-thinking writers and composers combine these same basic notes into fresh compositions. The beauty of the new can be experienced every day in the old simply by a creative rearrangement. Apply for a patent today by inventing something new out of the familiar.

What other combinations are there? A person could combine a sense of humor with an ability to write, to create stories or poems or plays. Or combine an interest in antiques with a handyman's ability to fix cars to begin a new hobby. Or couple a safe driving record with an interest in rally car driving to become involved in a new sport. Or merge a desire to be on stage with a natural ability in acting to join a community theater group. Or blend a capacity for understanding with an ability to care to reach out and help someone else. What interests, abilities, talents, and desires do you have? Combine them and create for yourself.

Yes, don't stop to just smell the roses. Taste, touch, see, and, yes, even hear the flowers. Enhance your ability to think creatively by experiencing a constant fresh view of life. When you do, you dig deeper into life's possibilities.

You are now ready for Step 4 of Creative Thinking. You are now ready to totally see and feel that every problem has a solution.

Step 4. A—Assume that Every Problem Has a Solution

While delivering a commencement address to an Ohio high school class, I turned to the graduates and relatives and asked, "How many of you think we can cure the world's hunger problems within the next five years?" Not one of the few thousand people present felt that the problem of world starvation could be solved. I looked at the graduates seated in the front rows and commented, "Do you see why some problems haven't been solved? When people don't believe that there are solutions, they don't look for them. Yet, every single problem has many, many possible solutions. Answers play hide-and-seek with us. As a child, when you played hide-and-seek, did you give up even before you looked? Or did you look only once or twice before you called your buddy out of the shadows?" I went on by telling the black-tasseled graduates, "I sure hope that one of you believes that somewhere out there in the world's hideouts lies the solutions to the great problems facing humanity. Jonas Salk played hide-and-seek with the cure for the disease of polio and found it. Thomas Edison believed that somewhere there existed a better way to read than by candlelight and went on to find a way. Yes, there are answers to every single problem. All you need is the determination to find them."

1. *Face life's challenges with the conviction that there is not only one answer, but many answers to every problem.* In fact, there are as many solutions to problems as there are people in the world.

2. *Be open-eyed as you glance in awe at everything about you.* Refrigerators, bathtubs, candles, baseballs, kites, and glasses were at one time nonexistent. Creative people who perceived these things as needs had the courage to assume that a solution could be found for each need and thus went ahead to accomplish the tasks before them.

3. *Watch the power and help you receive when you proceed through the day convinced that your problems have solutions.* This positive conviction in itself moves you out of the starting gate and halfway toward any solution you are looking for. Spend your energies, not by discouraging yourself, but by taking creative mental leaps toward finding the answers.

4. *Be an inventor in your everyday life.* Watch how easy it is when you act on the assumption that there are ways to improve on things around you. Consider this common problem: "I spend too much money on gasoline." Watch how ineffective it is to conclude, "There is nothing I can do." If I believe there is no solution, I might use all of my energies parked on Angry Avenue griping about the world, big oil companies, service station owners, automobile manufacturers, etc. Result: the problem isn't solved. I still continue to spend too much money on gasoline.

Next, observe how another person who faces the same problem, but believes that there are answers, proceeds to deal with a budget. "My problem is I spend too much money on gasoline." The person living on

Success Street concludes, "I want to cut down $30 a month on my gasoline bill. I know it can be done. Let me develop a plan. First, I will get up a few minutes earlier two days a week to walk to work, and I will take the bus more often, which is cheaper than burning gas. Then I will make a fewer number of trips to the store by developing a more thorough grocery list, allowing me to buy more in bulk and less often. When I travel on longer trips, I will travel by bus or train instead of my car. I will pump my own gas and save a few pennies on each gallon, and I will also travel at 55 miles per hour to increase my gas mileage. All of these ideas just for starters!"

If, however, these answers are too timid for the more assertive person, how about this alternative plan? "I will write to my government representative and get my neighbors to do the same. I will see if I can enlist the support of my whole town to force some political action that will provide for bigger tax breaks to gasoline users. I will even get a part-time job maybe pumping gas!"

Whose approach is more effective, the one who concludes there is no answer or the one who knows there is?

Every problem can be dealt with in a similar way and each has many solutions. Remember, life's answers are playing hide-and-seek with you. In realizing that there are answers to all of your problems, you're half-way to finding the solutions. Now, build your courage, have faith in yourself, and let your ideas carry you closer to your goals.

Step 5. T—Trust Your Own Ideas

Do you remember a time when you didn't trust your own ideas? I do! Even today, I can recall a scene in my life when I was in the first grade with quite a creative teacher. Yes, I remember the shrewd mentor asking our class of little ones a question. But to grab our ears (I assume), she lassoed our attention by offering a challenge to us. She said, "I know that you boys and girls are only first graders, but today I'm going to ask you a real hard question. It is really a question for second graders, and I think that it is probably too hard for any of you first graders, but I'll ask you anyway."

The teacher's challenge put our little minds in full force. Though I don't recall her specific question, I do remember being amazed that I thought I knew the answer. At first I was excited, but a split second later I thought, "My answer must be wrong. How could I, a first grader, know the answer to a question for a second grader?" So I didn't trust myself, and I didn't raise my hand.

And you know what happened next, don't you? Right! Another courageous student raised her hand and gave the exact answer that I was thinking of. I'll never forget the teacher's reaction to the girl's answer. The schoolmarm enthusiastically responded, "Mary Lou, you are simply a genius. I'm even going to call the principal in and tell the principal what a bright girl we have in first grade." As I watched the principal pat Mary Lou on her back, I decided that I would trust my own ideas in the future.

Did that ever happen to you? Perhaps Mary Lou's answer could have been provided by anyone in the class, but Mary Lou was successful because she had a positive self-image which allowed her to trust her own ideas. Self-trust is more important to achieve success than intelligence!

My friend, the incredible E.T. Love, saw a need for a road to cross through the as-yet-underdeveloped mid-western portion of Canada in the 1940's. He faced constant opposition as he advanced his progressive notion. Many resisted, arguing that the profits that could be reaped from this formidable venture would not warrant the costs. Others saw this mission as almost impossible. Still other short-term thinkers felt that the existing railroad was all that was necessary.

Despite the resistance, E.T. Love knew the road was needed and could be constructed. He trusted his idea. The giant took his herculean idea and enlisted support from many others. Today the Yellowhead Highway spanning all of Western Canada proudly paves the way for thousands of travellers every year. As a result of his foresight and self-trust, millions of people each year experience the magnificence of a great variety of landscapes from the lakelands and prairies of Manitoba and Saskatchewan to the majestic and awe-inspiring beauty of Jasper, Alberta, the Canadian Rockies, and the woodlands of the British Columbia interior. E.T. Love not only accomplished his dream, he created dreams for millions of other people. He had faith in himself.

On self-trust, the psychologist Carl Rogers wrote:

El Greco must have realized as he looked at some of his early work that "good artists do not paint like that." But somehow he trusted his own experiencing of life, the process of himself, sufficiently that he could go on expressing his own unique perceptions. It was as though he could say, "Good artists do nòt paint like this, but I paint like this." Or to move to another field, Ernest Hemingway was surely aware that "good writers do not write like this." But fortunately, he moved toward being Hemingway, being himself, rather than towards someone else's conception of a good writer. Einstein seems to have been unusually oblivious to the fact that good physicists did not think his kind of thoughts. Rather than drawing back because of inadequate academic preparation in physics, he simply moved toward being Einstein, toward thinking his own thoughts, toward being as truly and deeply himself as he could. This is not a phenomenon which occurs only in the artist or the genius. Time and again . . . I have seen simple people become significant and creative in their own spheres, as they have developed more trust of the processes going on within themselves, and have dared to feel their own feelings, live by values which they discovered within, and express themselves in their own unique ways.

Trust your own ideas. They are yours. Your ideas are unique, and, like my first grade classmate Mary Lou, E. T. Love, El Greco, Hemingway, and Einstein, give your ideas all green lights in their travels to Success City.

1. *Remember, you are one of a kind.* If your ideas and the ideas of your boss, your spouse, or your friend are exactly alike, one of you becomes unnecessary. So trust your ideas. Your thoughts give you uniqueness and significance.

2. *Constantly ask yourself, "What do I really believe?"* Continually ask, "Am I living my life totally consistent with my beliefs? Have I been honest and up-front with other people about my beliefs or am I afraid to be a person?" Force yourself to be in harmony with yourself so that people know you as the unique you, instead of being merely an echo of the ideas of others.

3. *Trust your new ideas.* Every time a new idea occurs to you, let it flow and write it down immediately. Keep paper and pencil with you at all times, even when going to bed. A short pencil is more effective than even a long memory. Remember that success is built on ideas, and to miss one idea by either blocking it or not having the equipment to record it is a loss to the world. If you found yourself usually blocking new ideas up to now, change at this moment and become a spontaneous "let it flow" person. If you find yourself getting stale and rigid, please go back to the relaxation exercise earlier in this chapter.

4. *Assume every single idea has merit.* Some ideas have merit in themselves, but most creative thoughts are valuable because of their ability to generate further ideas. Great ideas are series of thoughts, not a single thought. Plant ideas, the seeds to success, and then each day give them water and sunshine.

Be yourself and trust your ideas. Next, add to your creative thoughts by being open to the ideas of others.

Step 6. I—Invite the Ideas of Other People

Remember, success is built on nothing more than IDEAS. And when you trust your own ideas, you can magnify your POWER by inviting new ideas from other people. Just as you create your mood by selecting one radio station's songs over another's, you can create your mood for ideas by selecting fresh idea people to listen to and brainstorm with.

1. *Be a "what-do-YOU-think" type person.* Learn to listen to people's ideas without immediately judging them. Criticism is the quickest way of nipping a successful idea in the bud. Patiently hear people through, and you will be amazed at how much you can learn from them. Even little people, two years old, have some great ideas.

2. *Invite the ideas of others by being a sit forward, head nodding, fully attentive person.* Use expressive words like great, fantastic, and incredible when you find their ideas great, fantastic, and incredible. Soon you will find that people will be sharing ideas with you that they would otherwise have kept to themselves.

One of the most successful people I have worked with is a vice-president for administration of a specialty steel company based in the U.S.A. Len Coleman rose up the ranks like a helium balloon under water from his original background in accounting.

His background in accounting was totally foreign from his V.P. responsibilities in providing special services to over 5,000 employees. One day, while employed as a consultant for the steel company, I shared lunch with Lenny. I asked him how it was that he achieved such huge success and markedly improved department morale without a background in administration or management.

The well-groomed enthusiast said that it was not difficult. Len replied, "My expertise is in helping everyone else to see their expertise. I try to create an uncritical atmosphere in which no idea is viewed as absurd, and the employees' ideas flow. When you get the ideas of 5,000 people working towards the good of the company, you greatly increase the ability of the company to progress. Being the only 'expert' may be good for my ego, but this unrealistic title depreciates the service of 5,000 others, which, in turn, reduces company morale and productivity. My success is simply a matter of efficient and creative thinking."

Len was truly a "what-do-YOU-think" person who was interested in what the other person had to say. He practiced what he preached. In fact, he urged me to talk and listened to my ideas for the rest of lunch. His attention felt good for me, and a week later he told me how he used some of my ideas on the job. He received some more "free" consulting time from me!

3. *Give people credit for their ideas and show them how their ideas contributed to your growth.* Inspire people by thanking them for their ideas, as Lenny Coleman did with me. President of the United States Ronald Reagan was often inspired by a quote that he kept on his desk. The plaque read, "There is no limit to what you can do or where you can go as long as you don't care who gets the credit."

4. *Listen to the ideas of others in books and music.* Be fully responsive and sensitive to the words in songs and in books. Every book and record is waiting to be invited into your space, and they are full of new ideas for you. Don't loiter your life away by missing the ideas before you. Think, at this very moment, of a new source of ideas which is available to you in your immediate environment!

Get refreshment from the ideas of other people. Other people can show you new ways of rearranging your mental furniture. And, again, their information is often free. While Archie Bunker ignores the "new" by always sitting in the same chair in his "dying" room and gets upset at "new" ideas, look for the free refreshment. Don't let your ideas become as stale as Archie's cigar smoke!

Remember, the person on the street is an expert in one area or another. While some airlines have experts to tell them why people fear flying, other airlines go right to the everyday passenger and ask, "What do you fear most about flying?" Free answers are awaiting you everywhere you go. Open up all of your mental doors to the ideas of other people. Let everyone who holds an idea see you with arms as wide open as the Statue of Liberty. When you assume that (1) there are many answers to every problem, (2) you trust your own ideas, and (3) you encourage other people to share their ideas with you, you come to the next step in Creative Thinking. Step 7 is the ability to visualize success.

Step 7. V—Visualize Your Success

In working with people in weight loss programs, I spend much of the time in the opening session emphasizing one particular point. The key point I make to these people who are anticipating the start of their "losing streak" is they must visualize themselves as thin even before their formal program begins. I ask the participants these questions: "Can you, at this moment, mentally see yourself as thin? Can you form a picture of yourself as appearing the exact way you would like to look? Can you visualize yourself going to the tailor to have your present clothing taken in? Picture it! Can you hear people compliment you about your new appearance and, without putting yourself down, actually say, 'Thank you'?

"If your self-image allows you to see yourself thin, you are halfway there. If, however, you cannot picture yourself in this new 'light,' it is best to save your time and money and leave the program in this first session."

As perhaps you will recall, in Chapter II Prescott Lecky showed how we strive to be consistent with our self-images. If you see yourself as a "heavy person," your heavy self-image will play all sorts of games with you to keep you heavy. You will find yourself saying things like, "Well, it's okay to eat this cake and ice cream because it's my birthday," or, "I'll eat this spaghetti tonight, but I will work doubly hard on my diet tomorrow." Yes, the self-image is powerful enough to subconsciously talk you into staying heavy.

But the good news is that if you can picture yourself thin, you will succeed in losing weight. When your self-image sees yourself as a "thin person" in a heavier body, you will become the real you. If you can see success, you can achieve success.

The great football coach, Bob Devaney, turned the University of Nebraska, a continual loser on the field, into an annual winner. Tens of thousands of red-outfitted Cornhusker fans can be seen almost every January 1st watching their team performing in a bowl game. How did he achieve this monumental task? The coach focused on helping the members of his team visualize themselves as winners.

Can you recall moments in your life when you pictured yourself eventually achieving a certain goal? That ability to visualize success prepares every part of your mind and body to walk, talk, and even think like a success. And soon success is yours.

1. *Visualize success.* Try it with people. At an airport, in a waiting room, or on a bus, extend a few kind words to a person near you. But prior to starting the conversation, picture that the few words will lead to a longer conversation. Imagine the two of you are really hitting it off. Literally see, in your mind's eye, yourself finding much in common with this stranger. At the exact moment that you feel it finally begin, watch the results!

2. *When you are "down in the dumps," use your positive self-image to visualize yourself as "high and up" on life.* How would you look? How would you act? What would you do? If you can visualize yourself successfully overcoming your low feelings, your spirits will rise at that moment. When you change your picture of yourself, your thoughts and

feelings change. Instead of gloomy thoughts, your self-image concludes, "I'm going to develop a positive plan and then act on it. First, I will call a friend . . . ." There you go; you're on your way.

3. *Each night write a positive horoscope for yourself for the next day.* Predict the events of the next day and make sure your self-image sees the events as possible. I learned this idea from Elaine, one of my clients. She developed her horoscope and placed it beside her alarm clock so that she could read it immediately upon waking up. She wrote:

My Horoscope for Today

Today is my day, all the way. At this exact moment, I am the youngest age I will ever be. Here, in my youth, I am free. I am free today to brighten up people's lives or drag people down. Today I will choose to lift everyone's spirit. Today, as every day, I will run into barriers, but somehow or another I will be able to look at the obstacles as challenges and deal with them head on. Today I will dress my best, look my best, feel my best. Yes, I have the feeling that today will be owned by me all the way. My only regret is that there are only twenty-four hours to this one.

My client imparted to me a week later that she felt so good on this day that she telephoned a relative that she hadn't spoken to in 11 years. They set up a date to have dinner at Elaine's house. My client told me, "My positive horoscope worked so well for me that day that I decided to use it again the next day!" Interestingly, Elaine later glanced, out of curiosity, at her "real" horoscope. It read, "Do not take any personal or business risks today. This is a dangerous day for you to spend time with people. Today, however, would be a great day for writing, reading, and sedentary activities."

Elaine made her own stars, and the day twinkled for her because she visualized personal success. What your self-image sees, it will become. Visualize success and it is yours. Next, make a commitment to achieve that success.

Step 8. I—Ink Your Contract With Yourself.

After your self-image visualizes the success that you know exists, it is time for you to make your MENTAL MOVE. A MENTAL MOVE is your contract with yourself, a commitment to action. You ink your contract when you "draw up your will." Not your legal will, but your determination will.

You have decided to change a part of you. You have dreamt of the possible. You have experienced a wide and open view of the world. You trusted yourself and invited the ideas of other people. You visualized success. Now it is time to make a commitment.

Make a contract with yourself by writing five different headlines for yourself telling what you will achieve, by when, and what you will start on today. Remember, use the powers of creative thinking to develop your headlines.

1. *Write a headline for yourself that announces the successful achievement of your physical fitness and appearance goals.* Keeping the confines of your basic physical features in mind and realizing that you are a beautiful human being as unique as anyone, visualize how you can improve on what you already have. Dream; visualize yourself as your ideal self. (Pause.) Set a date to achieve your goal. Lock the picture of your desired physical self and your date of achievement firmly in your mind. Make a commitment. Ask yourself, "What can I do right now to start?" And each night reaffirm your commitment by asking yourself, "What can I do tomorrow in order to fit in with my goal?" Success is yours if you follow this pattern for a few minutes every day.

2. *Write a headline for yourself that shouts about your achievement of your financial goals.* How much will you earn by the date you list in your headlines? Visualize yourself earning that amount. Calculate what a monthly paycheck will be when you reach this financial goal. What can you do to start achieving this goal? Again each night, set aside a few minutes to plan how you can get closer to your goal tomorrow. Make a commitment to achieve it.

3. *Write a headline for yourself that announces to the world how you will be seen socially.* How would you like other people to view you? What traits or characteristics would you like to have? Set a date in your mind. Visualize yourself as being the type person that you desire to be. Make a commitment to yourself that you will achieve this goal. What can you do today to start? Become determined to spend a few seconds with yourself each night to plan how you will get closer to your goal the next day.

4. *Write a headline for yourself listing a certain date by which you will achieve an important professional, educational, or recreational goal.* What do you want to achieve—really achieve—in your professional, educational, or recreational lifetime? Make a commitment to start by listing a practical beginning point right now. Again, become determined to review your goal each night and plan for the next day.

5. *Write a headline for yourself stating that you have achieved a certain spiritual goal.* Let the headlines proclaim a relationship you would like to have with God, life itself, the universe, or whatever is spirit-

ual to you. What can you do at this moment to start toward your success? Plan, as always, to think about your next day's goals each evening.

Now ink your contract by signing it and referring to it each day. Your commitment will turn your creative thoughts and dreams into action. Next, take positive action towards your goals.

Step 9. T—Take Positive Action

You are known, in the end, only by your actions. Many a lover has been disappointed by the smooth words, plans, and even "genuine" commitments of another. Words, plans, and commitments are easily said, but "action speaks louder than words" and is the only effective way of starting on the pathway to success. If you want to truly know a person, watch what he or she does and not what he or she says. In fact, a universe of well-intentioned ideas is not the equivalent to one step in a positive direction. Only actions count. "Know thyself," Socrates said, and to know yourself, don't listen to what you say you'll do; watch for what you actually do.

1. *Practice being an action person.* Keep your promises to people. Go out of your way to be on time for every meeting. Being late is not so much a disrespect for time as it is a disrespectful action toward people.

The personnel manager of a container drum company told me how he hired his salespeople. Bill said, "When the applicants are reduced to two or three, I set up a couple more brief appointments with each of the remaining candidates. I observe who makes it on time. If someone is late, I eliminate his or her name from the successful candidates for employment list. It may sound cold, but I accept no excuses for lateness. If there is a traffic jam, the responsible person considers that possibility ahead of time. Being on time is an important trait and is a much better gauge of whether someone will be successful than the person's ability to make excuses. Action, not words, are what I want."

2. *Act even if you anticipate that your actions may not be perfect.* Overcome the disease of perfectionism. The major symptom of this disease is a fear of action. Perfectionists spend their energies contemplating the hazards of making a mistake rather than experiencing the joy of growing. Mistakes are to learn from. Develop what the psychiatrist Rudolf Dreikurs called "the courage to be imperfect." Interestingly, research points out that salespeople who are perfectionists earn much less each year than salespeople who have the courage to make a mistake. The latter group takes action risks in making calls without the fear of failure.

3. *Find a balance between planning and action.* Compulsive people are over-planners. They spend their energies looking down the road developing one-year, five-year, ten-year plans, which is great, but unfor-

tunately they don't act. There is safety in planning. Contrarily, impulsive people are always acting on a whim and are disorganized since they have no plan and no goal. Find a nice harmony between your plans and your actions—both are necessary.

4. *Don't wait for "just the right moment" to act.* If you plan on calling on an account, or changing your hairstyle, or going back to school when "the right moment" occurs, you may never act. Life gives no guarantees that your actions will be successful, but life does give you more chances. The right moment is now!

Remember, you can only know yourself by your actions, not your plans or intentions. You pay for the number of drinks you had, not how many you planned to have. Take action on your creative thoughts and commitments, and watch the 99% who stand on the sidelines. Success is yours through action.

The whole process of creative thinking starts with a willingness to challenge your ideas, to look for new ideas without fear, to know that there is more for you in life, to trust yourself and learn from the ideas of others, and to develop a plan and to act on that plan. The last step of Creative Thinking is the willingness to yield to even newer ideas.

Step 10. Y—Yield to New Creative Ideas.

The late psychologist Abraham Maslow, well-known for his studies on the healthiest human beings or self-actualized people, found that creativity was a key element in any healthy lifestyle. In fact, Maslow pointed out that no idea is good unless it brings forth a new one. It was true that self-actualized people did not have a need to say, "Aha, this is it. The idea is complete and I will live by it forever." Contrarily, they would see an idea as only a seed, a tentative thought, and never a finished product. Make certain that you don't get so caught in an idea that you can't see ways of improving on it.

John Lennon, one of the most influential song writers of all times, touched the lives of literally hundreds of millions of people. This was certainly reason enough for John Lennon to stay with his early ideas since they obviously were successful. But while on top, John Lennon made major shifts in his thinking. He trusted himself to yield to new ideas. His change produced a negative outcry from many of his fans because they needed to be able to "predict" him. But Lennon's mind was growing and yielding to new ideas. In fact, as you know, he even gave up his career to yield to the new idea of being a husband and father. By doing so, John Lennon lived his shortened life to its fullest. He lived in creation, not defense of past ideas.

1. *Yield to new ideas.* When you are ready to make a commitment to act, make it fully and act on the commitment completely. After the action is over, however, evaluate it and be open to yield to the new ideas that you gained along the way.

2. *At that exact moment when you think you know it all, it might be a clue that your idea system needs a checkup.* Times change, conditions change, and ideas that have worked before may not necessarily work again. Remember how you perhaps argued with absolute certainty the "fact" that the literal Santa Claus really existed? Give your idea system constant checkups by yielding to new ideas.

A friend of mind had the misfortune of losing his wife while they were only in their early forties. After the usual period of remorse, he started to see a few other women. Dating singles was a "far out" experience for Jon, whose ideas of relationships were based on his past married life. The music that he and his wife listened to didn't "turn on" his new dates who were more interested in modern music. His clothing, while quite appropriate for another era, was the source of open humor. He was affectionately called an "old timer." His ideas that were appropriate at one time were now outdated. Jon, being an intelligent man, instead of thinking that the whole world should shift to meet his ideas, decided to yield to new ideas. His self-image could visualize himself in new clothing, reading modern books, and listening to new music. In fact, whenever I see Jon, he tells me about some of the latest singing groups, stimulating my interest in new music. Today, Jon is remarried and both he and his wife are committed to new experiences, new ideas, and a fuller life. Like Jon, throw out your mental scrubboard and yield to the new ideas of living, dreaming, and thinking.

3. *Reverse your aging process by yielding to new ideas.* Become determined that you will defeat that tendency in you that suffers from what the popular educator, Zac Clements, calls the "in-my-day" disease. Patients living in the "in-my-day" dorm spend their energies decrying the present and glorifying the past. They argue that everything was better back then. The "in-my-dayers" shout about how much tastier the food was back then. (In fact, for them it was. Aging affects the taste buds, and the older the person is, the more likely the person is unable to experience some tastes that could be experienced at a younger age.) They talk about how well people behaved "in my day." But think of it. Even if they are totally correct that things were better in their day, so what! The world isn't "back then" and their desire to ride the time machine back into the past cannot be fulfilled except in their own minds. Become invigorated by

giving yourself the ultimate present, "a present of the present." Yes, "get off your past and get to the task. Give a hooray for the fact of today!"

Yield to new creative ideas, and a positive growing self-image and a refreshing new life is yours.

EXPANDING YOUR SELF-IMAGE THROUGH CREATIVE THINKING

Remember, success is built on nothing more than ideas. If your ideas of today are exactly the same as your ideas of yesterday, you have just wasted a day. Live every day in new creative and exciting ways. Give a lift to the ordinary by making it extraordinary. Experience all of the colors, sounds, and sights in the world. Rearrange your mental furniture with your powers of creative thinking.

THE DISTANCE FROM THE "IMPOSSIBLE" TO THE "POSSIBLE" IS ONLY TEN STEPS

Memorize the Ten Steps to Creative Thinking, and whenever your thoughts are fogged in the Valley of the Impossible, take the steps, rise above the clouds, and climb to the Pinnacle of the Possible.

Step   1. C—Challenge yourself to change.
Step   2. R—Relax and daydream of the possible.
Step   3. E—Experience a constantly fresh view of life.
Step   4. A—Assume that every problem has a solution.
Step   5. T—Trust your own ideas.
Step   6. I —Invite the ideas of others.
Step   7. V—Visualize success.
Step   8. I —Ink your contract with yourself.
Step   9. T—Take positive action.
Step 10. Y—Yield to new ideas.

Now give your powers of creative thinking the fuel to succccess—Enthusiasm.

CHAPTER IV

Igniting Your Enthusiasm: The Power System to Success

Get your winning streak started! Mix your unlimited supply of creative ideas with the most powerful fuel in the universe—enthusiasm—to create a never-failing formula for success. Spread this formula of Creative Thinking (CT) and Enthusiasm (E) wherever you go, and there's no stopping you and your scale to the summit. Always remember: CT + E = an unbeatable ME!

Enthusiasm provides the power for you to reach Success City. The enthusiasts are the ones who go the extra mile, who are high on life, who are enjoyable to be around, and who make the world more positive. You can further develop your own self-image through the power of enthusiasm. Enthusiasm is constantly with you and can be drawn on any time you need it, just by changing the way you look at things.

BECOME YOUR OWN OPTOMETRIST: MAKE A DECISION TO CLEAR YOUR VISION

It's all in the way you look at things! If your power system, your zest for life, is turned off, you can easily ignite the engines again by changing your attitude. Become your own optometrist today and put on an enthusiastic set of eyeglasses in order to view yourself, other people, and the world in a new way.

The philosopher, William James, proclaimed that the greatest revolution of the century was the discovery that human beings, by changing their inner view of themselves in their minds, could change the outer characteristics of their lives. Think of it. By changing the way you look at things, through your new set of eyeglasses towards life, you can actually change your life. The incredible story of William James, surely one of the most popular philosophers of all times, is a perfect example of the power of a person's view of life.

James suffered from severe depressions and was even suicidal at times. James, like many people today, pondered the uselessness of his life, often seeing no reason to go on. He believed that nothing seemed to really matter. James felt that it was useless to work harder at life if nothing really mattered anyway.

In a letter to a friend, James expressed his hopeless, "what's-the-use" view of things. He described his fatalistic outlook on life and his belief that everything was predetermined. The return letter from his friend literally changed the academic world for decades just by changing James's view of life. In this significant letter, James's friend urged him to believe in himself, just for one day, only to see how making a commitment to happiness could actually bring about happiness.

James took his friend's advice. The next day, James started his winning streak by changing his view of the day. Instead of believing that he was powerless and had no control over his life, James acted as if he did. He concluded that it was up to him to develop a productive, hopeful view of life. This outlook literally gave him the enthusiasm (the power system) necessary to meet the challenges of the day. With his new life outlook, or "inlook," his life changed dramatically, and, with his new power system, William James began making monumental contributions to the disciplines of philosophy and psychology. In fact, James went on to develop one of the major schools of philosophy, the philosophy of pragmatism. Not coincidentally, pragmatism is the idea that "truth is simply the process of finding beliefs that work." His previous hopelessness and negative beliefs about life didn't work. They didn't help him to succeed. However, when James made a commitment each day to become enthused about his life and profession, the new enthusiastic belief worked and he succeeded. James became his own optometrist and changed his set of eyeglasses towards life, and his life changed. So why should you look at the world out of enthusiastic colored glasses? Only because it works! And can you think of a better reason to be enthusiastic than that?

ENTHUSIASTS DEVELOP LIFE OUTLOOKS THAT WORK

The poet Samuel Johnson wrote, "When there is no hope, there can be no endeavor." Hopelessness and lack of enthusiasm keep the down times seething. But hope and enthusiasm are the fuels to power you past any cloudy weather. Be a rocket ship shooting for the stars by putting enough of these energy sources into your power system. With hope and enthusiasm, you can rise above clouds and into the space where the sun never stops shining.

Feel the power of an enthusiastic outlook. It is even more powerful in producing success than is intelligence. In the late 1970's, I was invited to participate in a noontime TV program to debate with one of the most brilliant people I had ever met. The controversial dialogue centered on the topic of "Life in the 70's: The Greatest or Worst Time Ever to Live?" Prior to the 20-minute debate, I had the opportunity to spend a bit of time in the studio waiting room with my debate opponent, an advocate of fatalistic foundations. Even in the waiting room, his face wore a bitter, hopeless expression. To break the ice, I asked my opponent, among other questions, how long he thought that he could talk about how abominable life in the seventies was. He told me that he could probably expound forever about all of life's injustices, economic atrocities, political pilferings, natural disasters, education's inefficiencies, and moral decay. The Genius of Gloom went on to say that he had accumulated enough data to suggest that we would have been better off if we had never been thrust into the human cavalcade.

At that point, a few minutes away from the actual debate, I glanced at my opponent's reams of discouraging data. Not having a single jotting or fact to support my positive position, I felt a surge of unpreparedness. Because it was obvious that he had more information to present than I did, I offered my friend the opportunity to take some of my 10-minute debate time, along with his 10, to present his position. Without hesitation, he agreed to take not only his debate time, but to use five minutes of my time. I would have the last five minutes to express my positive view of the seventies.

A few moments later, it was time for the debate to begin. The host explained the unusual procedure the debate was to follow and then introduced the purveyor of the pessimistic perspective. The professor's presentation commenced, and in only a few seconds it was obvious that he was well versed in his topic. His data was impeccable, his content was well-organized and his delivery was congruent with the facts. His topic on how life was channeled onto a catastrophic course was so effective that I do have to admit at moments in his monologue I felt misery, hopelessness, despair, and even apathy towards life. In fact, I think that he presented enough data to justify contemplating my own suicide. That's how good his presentation was!

My time arrived. I took part of it to commend him for his eye-opening facts about life. I told him that I had no doubt that everything he said was a fact beyond question. Since I had not prepared a formal position, I closed by asking my opponent a question. I asked the man who attempted to bronze the gold medal of life, "Sir, does the view that you choose to give to your life make you happy and does it make you productive?"

To the successful, this is the only question. Do you have a view of life that "works" or do you have a view of life that "doesn't work." The important realization is not how intelligent you are, but rather how you can use your I.Q. to make things better. Using your intelligence as the professor did, to gather data about how bad things are, is unproductive busy work and certainly cannot make you happy. All of the negative data about life that can be amassed is sterile in the mind of a positive enthusiast who believes things can get better and proceeds to make things happen. The professor's ideas were accurate, but they didn't work. Find an outlook on life that works and make a difference by becoming enthusiastic.

Anyone interested in the history of humankind knows that there were always problems to challenge the human mind. And there were always people (most, in fact) who responded to these problems by griping, whining, complaining, or giving up. And then there were the others who saw the same problems and fired up their enthusiasm, hope and determination and looked for solutions. And it is a simple fact that the whole human lot has progressed because of these rare enthusiasts who, despite the odds, rejected the useless course of worrying, or wallowing in the deadend course of pessimism. That's why you see no streets in the world named after pessimists. Yes, humankind has progressed because of a few enthusiasts who faced the human challenge.

Such a positive doer was the famed Terry Fox. The young, handsome Canadian lad at the height of his athletic career was told that he had cancer in his right leg. The disease was rapidly spreading toward other parts of his body, forcing the need to amputate his leg. The sudden news shattered Terry's original lifetime dreams. But did Terry Fox give up and blame life, other people, or the world and run away? Not on your life! Instead of running away, the enthusiastic lad began the "Marathon of Hope" to help raise funds for cancer research. He took on the challenge of literally running, with the assistance of an artificial leg, from eastern to western Canada, a distance of over 3,000 miles. Unfortunately, Terry didn't succeed in reaching Vancouver because the cancer in his leg spread to his lungs and eventually to the rest of his body. After running halfway across the continent, he was hospitalized and shortly thereafter died. But Terry Fox did succeed in other ways. He not only raised millions of dollars for cancer research, he inspired all Canadians and people of other countries with the truth—"We can overcome." He made us realize that we all count. He brought people together to work toward common goals, and he brought the goodness out in us all. "Somewhere the hurting must stop," Terry Fox said. Cancer will be beaten one day because of people like Terry. Yes, THE ENTHUSIAST ALWAYS HAS A LEG TO STAND ON.

Another enthusiastic doer was Irwin Westheimer. The year was 1903. While at work one morning, the twenty-three-year-old man glanced through his office window and observed a young boy searching through the garbage can for food. Irwin Westheimer was touched, but, more importantly, he was determined. The pessimist might dissertate and decry the social injustices or even envision the doom of humankind over an additional glass of wine. Not Irwin. He went out to find the boy and bring him to his office. Irwin fed the boy, went to his home to meet the boy's mother, and eventually found employment for her. But the young enthusiast didn't stop there. Irwin went to the members of his club and encouraged each of them to do the same with other impoverished youth in the community.

In 1980, at the age of 101, Irwin Westheimer died. Or did he? No, because he continues to live in the hearts of over a quarter of a million boys who are still being touched by his enthusiastic actions. These fatherless boys feel a sense of enthusiasm every time they catch a football or go for a hike with a "Big Brother." Irwin Westheimer was the founder of the Big Brothers of America. Surely thousands of people see or read about children eating out of garbage cans. But Irwin was a doer who saw the problem and moved enthusiastically towards a solution.

Enthusiasts are the people who make the positive difference. They rise above any difficulty and take a Goodyear blimp view of life. Be an enthusiast. Reach into your energy system and send out positive electricity wherever you go. Don't wait for enthusiasm to find you. Get psyched up. Carry a constant imaginary string around your little finger reminding you that you can deal with any situation by becoming enthusiastic and seeing hopeful alternatives.

Another enthusiast who made the difference was Marva Collins. She is a Chicago school teacher rooted in enthusiasm. Frustrated by the public schools, she formed her own, the Westside Preparatory School. Soon after her school opened, she had sixth graders reading at the college level. She threw away the "See Sue run" books and introduced her elementary school children to Shakespeare, Plato, Aristotle, Emerson, and other classic writers. A powerful achievement, isn't it?

Yes, but the achievement is even more powerful than that. You see, Westside accepts only those students who are either expelled or are failing miserably in the public schools. The student body at Westside is composed of children labelled either "mentally retarded," "incorrigible," or suffering from some form of "learning disability." Initially, Marva Collins used her own home on Chicago's "tough" westside as a classroom for her 18 pupils. In five years' time, she had 200 students (aged 4 to 14) and seven teachers housed in a school building with six classrooms. Westside currently has a waiting list of over 1,000 children. W. Clement Stone, the multimillionaire and positive mental attitude enthusiast, recently awarded Westside a grant of $50,000 to carry on its work. All this, because of one person. Marva Collins saw a problem, fired her enthusiasm and made the difference. Again, if she hadn't seen hope for the children, there would not have been any hope.

Where in your life have you given up hope? To the enthusiast, there is always hope. Fire up your power system NOW and, like Terry Fox, Irwin Westheimer, and Marva Collins, get high and shine up the gold medal of life.

Enthusiasm works. It makes the difference! And not only does it make a difference, but when you develop your enthusiasm, you automatically develop your positive self-image. And it is as easy as changing your eyeglasses!

DEVELOPING YOUR POSITIVE SELF-IMAGE THROUGH ENTHUSIASM

If you were to think of some of the characteristics the best teacher who ever taught you had, there is a good chance you would say that first and foremost this person was enthusiastic. If you think of the most encouraging person you ever met, you probably would say, among other characteristics, this person was enthusiastic. Even when reflecting on the most interesting person you ever met, you perhaps remember an aura of enthusiasm around him or her. Enthusiasm, a heightened energy level and an optimistic zest for life, is a characteristic developed by successful people. In fact, it is quite difficult to find extremely successful people who have not developed their self-image by developing their enthusiasm.

Yes, enthusiasts are people like Terry Fox, Irwin Westheimer, and Marva Collins who change the world. You, too, when fully fired up with enthusiasm have a positive impact on yourself, other people, and life itself. Every time you create a smile on someone's face, you have just changed the world! When you are enthusiastic, you are more appealing, more popular, more influential, and even more attractive. Watch two people, one of whom is physically attractive but has a dullness of face and eyes; then watch another person who perhaps is not as physically attractive as the first person, but who has an enthusiastic facial expression, a wide smile, bright eyes, and a sense of aliveness. With whom would you prefer to associate? Yes, enthusiasm makes you more attractive. The enthusiast literally lights up a roomful of people just by opening the door. The enthusiast gives hope to the hopeless, and energy to the dull.

It's no wonder that people who have a positive self-image are usually seen as being enthusiastic. It was originally thought that positive self-image produces enthusiasm, but the opposite is just as true. The simple fact is that not only does a positive self-image produce enthusiasm, but enthusiasm produces a positive self-image. That's right. If you follow closely these ideas in developing your enthusiasm, you can literally create a more positive self-image. And like a little snowball rolling down a snow-covered mountain gathering more mass, your enthusiasm gathers more enthusiasm. And off you go on your winning streak. Develop your positive self-image by igniting your never-failing powers of enthusiasm. Brace yourself and develop your enthusiasm by working on three different levels: (1) getting enthused about yourself, (2) getting enthused about other people, and (3) getting enthused about life.

GETTING ENTHUSED ABOUT YOURSELF, YOUR UNIQUENESS, AND YOUR TALENTS

You are literally a miracle! You are such a rare combination of the physical and spiritual that there is no one, anywhere in the world, exactly like you. You are so special that you have been given the greatest gift in the world—you were selected to be a human being. You are the owner of your body, your mind, your actions, your thoughts, and your feelings. Even your dreams are uniquely yours. And this is your moment in the history of our universe. You are alive, which gives you the power to draw up the blueprints for the kind of person you want to be.

Tap those human powers that you have by igniting the power of enthusiasm for yourself and your possibilities. In fact, you are your possibilities in the beginning stages, waiting to happen. Your success happens when you turn on your electrical power of enthusiasm. And how do you turn on that electricity? How do you become enthusiastic? Simple. To become enthusiastic, all you have to do is BECOME ENTHUSIASTIC! Does that sound too simplistic? It's true. You become enthusiastic by becoming enthusiastic. Watch how simple it is to develop a positive self-image by BECOMING ENTHUSIASTIC.

1. *Smile enthusiastically.* Wherever you go, watch the lifegiving power that your smile has on people. I have asked thousands of people the question, "Who would you rather be with, an enthusiastic person or a person with a frown?" Does it surprise you to discover that not one single person preferred a frowning person? Be the energy wherever you go. Even if at first it seems unnatural to extend a warm welcoming smile to everyone, it will soon be as natural to you as tying your shoes. To realize the power of a smile, just think of two people. The first person who never smiles, we'll call I. M. Dull. How do you feel around I. M. Dull? I. M. Dull isn't very rewarding to be around. Would you buy anything from I. M. Dull? Would you enjoy listening to a lecture from I. M. Dull? Probably not. Now consider another person, a good listener, who meets you with a warm smile. Let's call this person N. Thusiastic. Isn't N. Thusiastic a more refreshing person to be around? Doesn't this person give you more life than I. M. Dull? No wonder people with a smile have a more positive self-image. Remember, a smile creates a positive self-image. Get enthused about yourself. Become determined that you will light up the faces of people by your smile; then watch your self-image climb like a spaceship ascending from the launching pad at Cape Kennedy.

2. *Walk enthusiastically.* Enthusiasts walk faster. Why not? They are going places. Compare the walks of I. M. Dull and N. Thusiastic. While Dull walks with head down, shoulders curved inward, and with a short apologetic step, N. Thusiastic walks with head up (even in the rain), shoulders back, and with a crisp gait. Without meeting these two individuals, you draw conclusions about them, just by observing their walks. Their walks tell a story. Interestingly, research demonstrates that most victims of muggings tend to have a certain walk. Prisoners who were serving time for muggings agreed that a person's walk strongly influenced their decision to attack. The person most likely to become a mugging victim is one taking short, shuffling steps with the chest buried between the shoulders. Remember, your walk stems from your self-image, but your self-image stems also from how you walk. Change the way you walk. Walk like an enthusiast and soon a positive self-image will become part of you. Win people over even before you meet them by your confident, enthusiastic walk.

3. *Get psyched on yourself by speaking enthusiastically.* Modulate your voice. Every person can remember never-ending sermons in

church given by a monotonous speaker. Yet, the same words brought to life by an enthusiastic speaker can give energy to the group and make the talk more powerful. You remember teachers, as well, who gave no excitement to their lessons. Or perhaps you experienced a salesperson who went on to simply describe a house, a car, or even a living room set with no life. The enthusiast puts vitality into the talk. Hold people's attention by putting refreshment into everything you say. Say "Hello" with life. Say "Congratulations" with vigor. Say, "Have a great day," with meaning and genuine enthusiasm. When you "vitalize" things, something interesting happens. You actually invigorate yourself. When someone asks you how you are doing, do you just say, "Okay," or "Not so good?" Enliving your response and watch how you can change your "okay" or "not so good" to "Terrific!" or "Fantastic!" You actually do become terrific or fantastic just by saying and feeling it.

4. *Use a vocabulary filled with enthusiastic words.* More and more psychological research is demonstrating the power of words on a person's emotions. If you think of it, depressed people tend to have a vocabulary filled with gloomy, inactive, depressing words. Contrarily, enthusiasts tend to have vocabularies overflowing with positive, active, assertive, enlivening words. Two prominent behavioral scientists, Albert Ellis (co-author of *A Guide to Rational Living*) and Charles Zastrow (author of *Talk to Yourself*) show how we create our emotions simply by the words we use. Change your life and your self-image by changing your vocabulary. Compare the vocabularies of our friends I. M. Dull and N. Thusiastic.

Failure vs. Success Vocabulary

I. M. Dull says:	but	*N. Thusiastic says:*
"Things are awful, terrible."		"We face an exciting challenge."
"I hate aging."		"I love aging. After all, what is the alternative?"
"I'm way too old to change."		"My experiences give me an advantage in changing."
"Maybe it can be done."		"It absolutely can be done. I know the way to make it work."
"Things are okay."		"Things are great."
"Let's give up. It's no use."		"Okay, let's put ourselves into second gear."
"Good job."		"Fantastic performance."

"There are no answers." | "We have plenty of alternatives. Let's look for the best one."

"I've tried calling on that account before. They are too stubborn. Don't waste your time." | "I found one approach that didn't work on that account. Let's brainstorm and think about what the account needs and win it over."

Like the enthusiast, build your self-image on a foundation of strong, positive words. If you do, your emotions will change before your eyes. With a positive vocabulary and positive emotions, you become a powerful magnet, attracting positive people and success.

5. *Wake up enthusiastically.* In the morning, while most people treat their alarm clocks like the enemy, look at your alarm clock as though it were a friendly fire alarm. When it rings, jump out of bed fired up with your enthusiasm. Put a glow in your mind and your heart. An enthusiastic start to the day gives you an advantage over the ho-hum person who needs an hour and a morning cup of coffee or a morning smoke to get going. Let your fire alarm ignite action and enthusiasm for the day. Yes, the way to become enthusiastic is simply to BECOME ENTHUSIASTIC.

6. *Answer your phone enthusiastically.* Get off automatic pilot and get enthused every time the phone rings. Remember, the person calling is a person who has taken the time to dial you. Let the person catch your enthusiasm right from the start. While the programmed robot says a dull "Hello," the enthusiast answers with a cheery "Good afternoon," or, "Top of the morning to you," or even, "With a little good news from you, this could be both of our days." Develop new enthusiastic ways of answering the phone every day by letting your creativity flow. Your opening words on the phone are only limited by your creativity.

7. *Listen enthusiastically.* Win people over by employing the rarely used skill of enthusiastic listening. As you listen to people talk, lean forward. Use open, expressive eyes, conveying full attentiveness to the speaker's ideas. The world's best salespeople are not only great, enlivening speakers with positive vocabularies, but enthusiastic listeners as well. Stay away from playing games like "Can you top this?" or "That reminds me of my experiences. Let me tell you about them." Stay on their topic and watch your popularity soar! (For further information, see Chapter VIII, Leadership.)

8. *Build your self-image by constantly analyzing your assets.* While most people are more talented at seeing what is wrong rather than right with themselves, you should find only what's right with yourself. If you

have positive points and you don't recognize them, you are lying to yourself. Don't lie to yourself and the world. The world needs you to be a success, and to be a success, you have to focus on your strengths. Relax, sit back for a few minutes, and think about the following questions:

A) What have you accomplished that has given you real personal satisfaction? Include mental, parental, academic, social, physical, professional, financial, athletic, and spiritual accomplishments.

B) What do you consider to be your five most positive assets? (Don't move on until you find at least five.)

C) Think of the people you respect the most. What do you have in common with them? What do you have that they don't?

D) Think of some things you have done for other people that were really helpful to them during difficult times in their lives. Think, as well, about times when you helped someone to succeed with your encouragement.

E) What can you give in a personal relationship?

F) To whom could you really give a boost by giving a surprise call? What characteristic do you have that could give this person the boost?

G) Did you ever really want to achieve something, and after working hard for it finally succeed? Recall the experience and jot down all of the positive traits necessary for you to succeed.

H) Do you remember a time when you failed at something and, instead of giving up, came back stronger to overcome the failure? Relive the experience.

I) Recall a time when enthusiasm made the difference for you either in your personal or professional life. What happened? How did it feel?

J) What trait would you like to develop today? Combine your enthusiasm, your creative thinking, and your positive self-image, and "go for it."

Remember, a positive self-image is won by developing your enthusiasm. You become enthusiastic by BECOMING ENTHUSIASTIC. Get enthused about yourself by smiling enthusiastically, walking enthusiastically, speaking enthusiastically, building a vocabulary of enthusiasm, waking up and answering your phone enthusiastically, listening enthusiastically, and analyzing your assets every single day. When you do this, you are on your road to Success City via the Enthusiastic Expressway.

Now that you have become enthused about yourself, focus your attention on ways of Getting Enthused about Other People.

GETTING ENTHUSED ABOUT OTHER PEOPLE

Light the fires under everyone you meet with your enthusiasm. Pass on your positive energies and be a "pick-'em-up" type of person. Be easy to talk to and give people a warm feeling when they are with you. In a world that has too much loneliness and lack of caring, you can become a natural source of warmth, encouragement, and enthusiasm. Yes, enthusiasm makes the difference in your relationships with people.

How powerful is your enthusiasm in the lives of other people? Consider the following illustration of how the power of enthusiasm works. Imagine that while you are out shopping, you cross paths with some friends. During your conversation with them, they casually invite you to a party they are having the next day at their house. Perhaps you wonder whether they are sincere about the invitation. If so, you wonder why they did not invite you earlier if it was so important that you be there. Yet you really do want to go. All day you struggle with the decision to go or not to go. Lo and behold, the next day arrives, and bright and early that morning the telephone rings. It's your friends, and they again extend their invitation, enthusiastically saying, "We are really looking forward to seeing you tonight. We have so many things to talk about. Please try to come."

The extra effort on your friends' part may have enhanced the possibility that you would go to their party. Like this second effort, genuine enthusiasm is the skill of extending additional energies or heightened invitations to others.

1. *Get enthused about other people's lives.* Be a stimulant and not a depressant. Get excited about people's lives and work. Observe the different ways that I. M. Dull and N. Thusiastic listen to people.

Are You a Depressant or a Stimulant to People?

I. M. Dull says:

"You say you're writing a book? I understand that it is almost impossible to get a publisher nowadays. I had a cousin who was the top student in her class at Harvard in economics and she wrote a book and couldn't find a single publisher. All that work and nothing out of it. I personally don't think that writing a book is worth the effort."

"You're a hairdresser? I often wondered about you people. I would think that your job would get quite boring; one customer after another all day, just standing there cutting hair."

but N. Thusiastic says:

"You're writing a book? Wow, an author! I'll bet you're having a great time putting it together. You probably dream about it even in your sleep. And imagine the day that it comes out on the market and there's your name on the cover. Would you tell me a little about your ideas?"

"You're a hairdresser? Fantastic. It must be exciting to be in a profession where you help people to feel beautiful. You know, I've seen people who wouldn't be seen out in public until they saw their stylist.

You folks really do make the difference in people's lives. As I think of
it, why not? After all, people come to
you for more than just a styling.
They come to you for courage, confidence, and hope. It must feel good
being in such a rewarding profession."

Get enthused about people's lives and work. Be a stimulant and give them some of your energies.

2. *See what's right and not what's wrong with people.* Find the buried treasures, the hidden gold, in everyone. The difference in my life was made by a high school counselor who was a natural enthusiast and saw what was right with me. As I mentioned in Chapter I, I was a failing high school junior as a result of an extremely poor self-image. Most of my teachers attempted to motivate me by embarrassment, force, fear, intimidation, or focusing on my negative points. I recall an English teacher handing back to me a composition which contained many misspellings. As she handed my paper to me, she angrily proclaimed, "Losoncy, you are so stupid." I looked at her and couldn't understand her anger. I said, "I know I'm stupid, but why are you so angry at me being stupid. How are stupid people supposed to act—smart?" No, because stupid people act the only way they can act—stupidly! Every time we point out something negative in people, we carve the negative into their self-image. Remember, the self-image is the blueprint for their behavior!

The enthusiast in my life, my eleventh-grade high school counselor, knew how to be a stimulant and not a depressant. One day while walking down the hallways of good old Central Catholic High School in Reading, Pennsylvania, the counselor and priest stopped me in the hallway and touched me. He looked at me and enthusiastically said, "Lew, you are terrific." His positive comment was inconsistent with my negative self-image, and because the self-image seeks consistency, the praise was hard for me to swallow. My honest initial reaction to the comment was, "Do priests drink?" or, "I guess he wants me to set up chairs in the auditorium for the school assembly."

But I couldn't let go of this potential oasis of human nourishment in a desert of failure. I asked him, "You say that I am terrific, Father. What do you mean?" The bright-eyed priest turned to me and responded, "I just saw two nuns walking down the hallway, Lew, and you had them so upset they were actually cursing." Totally confused with his way of looking at things, I inquired, "Is that good?" The enthusiast responded, "It sure shows that you have a talent. You have a tremendous ability to influence people." He continued, "Have you ever thought about how you could use that ability?" With ears perked up, I responded, "No, not really." Father James Ferry, with genuine enthusiasm, gave me a few of the most meaningful moments of my life by telling me about all of the careers that would be available to a person like myself who has the ability to influence people. The opportunities of my life opened like the petals of a flower on a sunny day. Teaching, sales, politics, and many other careers were potentially in my crystal ball. My dreams were given back to me.

Who helped me more—the person who pointed out what was wrong with me, or the priest who saw beyond the negatives to the assets in me and helped me to reconstruct a positive self-image? Stimulants give hope, energy and purpose. Depressants give sermons, "shoulds" and discouragement.

Today, as I sit here typing this manuscript for you in my home located on an island off of the coast of the state of New Jersey, I reflect on the tremendous gift one enthusiast gave to me. I think about the fact that I have lectured on the ideas of success to hundreds of thousands of people throughout North America and have written a few books on the topics of encouragement, success, and positive attitude which have been read by over a quarter of a million people. I'm glad that the good priest, instead of giving me a sermon on that Tuesday morning, gave me a view of my assets. I hope, in a small way, I can be the James Ferry in your life by firing up your energies to see what's right and not what's wrong with you and other people. Peer through your positive spectacles and refuse to see the negatives without first seeing the positives.

Enthusiastically seeing what's right with people is especially important with people who are on a losing streak. They are the ones who really need your positive penicillin. I recall working as a counselor in an inner city elementary school. Each week a little first-grade girl, Heidi, would be sent to me to show me her spelling test paper. She was incredible. For almost three straight months, Heidi did not spell a single word correctly. She would show me her paper and say something like, "Mr. Losoncy, I got 10 wrong in my spelling again." The teacher, a depressant who marked the words Heidi spelled wrong, was giving Heidi the self-image of "poor speller." And how do poor spellers spell? Right! Poorly. Every Friday night, Heidi would be home writing, fifty times each, the words she misspelled that week. She hated spelling class, developed stomachaches before the test, and, like you and me, she didn't want to be at a place where she was going to fail.

Then the classic day arrived. One Friday in early December, Heidi brought her spelling paper to me, proclaiming, "Mr. Losoncy, I got nine wrong in my spelling." My mind immediately thought, "Nine wrong. There are ten questions. That means she spelled one correctly." I looked at the little first grader and asked to see her paper. As she proudly showed me her accomplishment, I looked at her and said, "Wow, Heidi, do you know that nobody in the whole wide world can spell that word 'cat' better than you?"

The pony-tailed tyke, reflecting on the ramifications of her achievement, looked at me and queried, "Nobody? You mean nobody in the whole wide world can spell 'cat' better than me?"

"That's right. Nobody in the world can spell 'cat' better than you." I paused for a second to let her absorb the statement and continued, "Understand, honey, there are a lot of people who can tie you in getting the word 'cat' spelled right, but nobody does it better than you."

The fires of enthusiasm caught her. She said, with real pride, "I'm pretty good at that word 'cat,' ain't I, Mr. Losoncy?" I enthusiastically responded, "That's right. You're good at the word 'cat,' and so you can be good at the words 'rat,' 'hat,' 'bat,' and all of the other words. You can do it."

I watched Heidi walk back to her room that afternoon ready to begin her spelling winning streak. In fact, later on in the afternoon, she brought me a little gift. She brought me a piece of paper with the word "cat" written on it 50 times just for me (although she misspelled my name on the paper). Get enthused about people. Be the rare stimulant who sees what's right with them and not what's wrong with them. (For a detailed analysis on techniques of motivating people, see Chapter VIII on Leadership).

3. *Work at remembering every person's name and a few important facts about him or her.* Assume that every person you meet, you will see again in the future. If you miss a person's name when you are introduced, force yourself to politely ask again. It shows that you are interested. Then say the person's name at least five times to yourself. Continually use his or her name when speaking to the person. This will reinforce your memory. Remember, people's names are the labels given to them by their mothers and fathers. Names are important, and when you open a conversation by using a person's name, that person gains a great deal of respect for you.

When you remember people's names, it starts off the next conversation you have with that person on a more meaningful level. Did you ever go to bed on a cold night and the sheets were freezing? You had to lie there for some time in the cold until your body warmed up the sheets, right? Forgetting a person's name makes you go through that warming-up period. Be a warm, cozy bedsheet for people by remembering their names and a few simple facts about them.

One of the most popular people I have ever met was the superintendent of schools in East Allen, Indiana. I was invited to speak to 500 faculty teachers who were under the supervision of the East Allen superintendent. Prior to my talk, the superintendent was introduced. He received a loud round of applause from the faculty. This is a rare happening because of the adverse relationship that generally builds between faculty and administration. After my talk, I asked a few faculty members why the superintendent had so much of their respect.

One teacher explained, "Dr. Yost is fantastic. He knows the name of not only every teacher in the school district, but their spouse's and children's names as well. In fact, Dr. Yost can tell you something positive about every one of his teachers. He rarely forgets a conversation." Success through memory.

4. *Get enthused about other people's claims to fame.* Something that N. Thusiastic knows that I. M. Dull doesn't know is the secret of getting enthused about people's accomplishments by their standards, not ours. I recall a conversation in a university lunch room that demonstrates this point. The dialogue was between a professor and Jeffrey, a student who apparently was not in this particular professor's class.

JEFFREY:	I received my grades today, and I got a "D" in my elements of geography class.
DR. LIVINGOOD:	I'm sorry to hear that news.
JEFFREY:	Why? I thought I was going to fail, which would have meant that I could not graduate in June. All I needed was the "D" to receive my university degree.

Dr. Livingood made the error of judging the student's accomplishment by a professor's standards. Perhaps the doctor was an "A" student throughout his complete schooling. Or perhaps he judged the student's accomplishment by more universal standards. In that case, a "C" is the average grade. Either way, the professor missed the opportunity to be a stimulant. He forgot to consider the grade from Jeffrey's point of view. Thus, he failed to recognize the great accomplishment: Jeffrey will be a university graduate.

Be sensitive to people's claims to fame. These claims to fame are proud accomplishments in people's lives and are meaningful to them even though to us or the rest of the world they may mean very little. I recall walking down the street one day and felt a little lad tugging at my clothing. The five- or six-year-old lad exclaimed, "Hey, mister, do you know what I can do?" I looked at the stranger decked out in baseball hat with the brim turned sideways and a boxful of Star Wars figures in his left hand and asked, "What can you do?"

The youngster replied, "I can turn the TV channel from 3 to 10 and hit it perfectly every time."

At first, I made the error of evaluating the little boy's accomplishment based upon its significance to the world and mechanically responded, "Good."

A few steps later, the child's feelings about his accomplishment were felt squarely in my mind and heart. What the child could do was for him so important that he stopped a total stranger to share his joy. Lighting my fires of enthusiasm towards the youngster's claim to fame, I returned to him and with vitality asserted, "Wow, you sure sound proud of what you can do with your TV set. I'll bet that took a lot of practice."

In our *Think Your Way to Success Seminars,* I spend much of my time helping participants sharpen their skills in claims-to-fame recognition. For example, it is of utmost motivational importance for a corporate executive to recognize the claims to fame of the employees in his or her organization. Or imagine the powerful impact a salesperson has as he or she walks in to see a client with "extended antennae" in search of the client's claims to fame. If you get enthused about people by recognizing their claims to fame and success, popularity and the power to influence are yours. Spend a few moments at this time thinking about the claims to fame of the people you see every day. Then do the most important thing you can do—enthusiastically share with them your recognition of their achievements. Does someone you know take pride in his or her ability to cook, to dance, to clean, to ride a bicycle, to add, to dress well, or to grow plants?

5. *Make it a point to help every person you meet to feel important and significant.* There is no greater need that people have than the need to "count." Apathy, low morale, stagnation, loneliness, and even suicide are symptoms of people who are basically saying, "I don't count. The world doesn't need me. It doesn't even matter whether or not I wake up tomorrow morning." Every person you see walking down the street, every person you meet at a social gathering, every person you work with has in common the need to "count." Enthusiastically count them in.

One of my close friends, Dr. Richard Cahn, knows as much about improving employee morale in an organization as perhaps anyone in the world. Dick, as of this writing, is superintendent of one of the larger school systems in the eastern United States. Dick was elected to his position during a time when the schools were facing several major problems, especially in areas of poor employee morale, excessive professional "burnout," and seemingly irreversible financial problems. Very few people would even want that challenge. However, Dick loves a challenge and is one of the most naturally enthusiastic people you could meet. He met the challenge squarely and in only one year—that's right, one year—turned the school district into a place where teachers wanted to be, where students took pride in being, and where new ideas flowed like the winds of Wyoming. It was the first time that a teacher contract was signed before the beginning of the school year (incidentally, it was also a three-year contract!).

How did Dick achieve these herculean accomplishments? Dick, in a humble tone, would tell you, "Working with people is the easiest task in the world if you just remember what makes people tick. People need to count, to feel a part of the organization, and to see that they make a difference. When I'm with a person, that individual is the only important person in the world and I have nothing else on my mind. Nothing else matters at that moment."

Employing enthusiasm and encouragement in his organization, Dick bubbles as he shares his beliefs about people in general. The master builder of morale reflects, "It has been my observation that most people are more fulfilled by performing well rather than by performing poorly, by contributing rather than by being uncooperative, and by feeling recognized rather than by feeling insignificant. People can find this fulfillment when an encouraging atmosphere exists. When we enthusiastically look for the best in people, we more often than not get their best. The indisputable principle of encouragement is, 'What you see is what you get.'"

Yes, when you get enthused about people, you turn them on and you reap the rewards of seeing their fires for life lit again. Be a stimulant by (1) getting enthused about other people's lives; (2) seeing what's right with people; (3) remembering every person's name and a few facts about the person; (4) recognizing every person's claims to fame; and finally, (5) helping every single person to feel significant and to have the "I count" feeling.

After putting on your positive enthusiastic spectacles and getting enthused about yourself and other people, develop your self-image even further by getting enthused about life today and learning to appreciate the beauty that surrounds you.

GET ENTHUSED ABOUT LIFE!

Celebrate today! We are now living in the greatest time ever. People perched on the porch of pessimism selectively perceive only the negative. They suffer from perceptual myopia, a disease characterized by the symptoms of negativism and blame. They miss all of the great news dancing in front of their eyes. They miss the fact that probably three and one-half billion out of the four and one-half billion people in the world would trade places with them in a moment's notice. What's worse, they miss making the best of their lives and being who they can be. Put on your enthusiastic glasses and not only get high on yourself and other people, but on life itself.

Instead of life today, would you rather be fighting dinosaurs? Would you prefer coping with freezing weather by rubbing two sticks together just to get a fleeting spark. If you would prefer getting warm that way, I have great news—you still have that option! Instead of the conveniences of life today, would you prefer having your bathroom an outhouse? Would you rather use a scrub board to clean your clothing?

Would you rather have the mobility we enjoy today or be restricted to "Shank's Pony" as the only form of transportation? Again, you still have most of these options available to you. However, though modern conveniences may not be the answer to everything, they certainly make life more comfortable and allow you more time for your loved ones, church, business, and/or leisure.

People who glorify the past are selective in their visions. They choose the positive elements from their imaginary ideal but ignore most of the dismal aspects about the past. So, enthusiastically click your heels together and rejoice about the beauty of life by seeing what's right and not what's wrong with the present. You are living in the greatest time ever and things are going to get even better. Because of enthusiasts, we are only a few years away from a pill that will enable you to eat anything that you want without gaining a single pound. We are a short time away from a nasal spray that will enhance your memory. Because of optimists, we are only a brief period of time away from taking partial control of some forms of destructive thundershowers and hurricanes. We are only a little calendar distance from the time when the average human being will live to be 100. And soon we will have control over most forms of tooth decay. For a further detailed analysis of how fantastic our future looks, please take some time to read *Breakthroughs* by the famous scientific writer Charles Panati.

And remember, not one of these breakthroughs came from the mind of a pessimist. Rejoice about the beauty of living in today's world and shout about the even greater beauty of living in tomorrow's world. Enthusiasm is the only way to go to achieve success. Reach Success City by developing your positive self-image fueled by enthusiasm.

A LIFETIME OF SUCCESS IS YOURS WITH CREATIVITY AND ENTHUSIASM

Success is the product of the creation of new ideas combined with the enthusiasm it takes to make these ideas happen. You can achieve any goal and succeed at anything you do just by continuously reminding yourself to see things in refreshing ways and to become enthusiastic about life, other people and, mainly, yourself.

Don't just saunter through life. Step through your day with a brisk pace. Own your life. Make things happen. When you get high on life, you can change the world. Imagine what could be accomplished in just one day of your life with the powers of your enthusiasm.

In one day, you could have breakfast in New York City, lunch in Vancouver, British Columbia, and settle down for a roast pig dinner in Honolulu.

In one day, you could travel one-seventh of the way to the moon. But if you don't have a full two weeks to spend travelling to and from the moon, wait. In the oncoming years, it will take even less of your valuable "alive" time.

In one day, you could produce the beginnings of a new life.

In one day, you could put a smile on hundreds of faces.

In one day, Mother Theresa, the Nobel Peace Prize winner, feeds tens of thousands of children in India.

In one day, in fact, in only seven seconds, the pit crew at an Indianapolis 500 race can change all of the tires on a car.

Yes, ignite your enthusiasm—the power system to success. Think of the possibilities you have in just one day when you are enthusiastic. What could you possibly do with your unlimited talents, unlimited assets, unlimited creative ideas, unlimited enthusiasm, in only one day? Well, brace yourself; not only do you have one of these days available to you, you probably have thirty thousand or more of these days available in your lifetime.

Remember,

$$CT + E = \text{an unbeatable ME.}$$

Next, apply your formula of creative thinking and enthusiasm to your goals to give them the pulling power they need to take you to Success City.

ENTHUSIASTIC REMINDERS—LIVE TODAY LIKE IT WAS YOUR FIRST . . . IT IS!

1. Enthusiasm is not something a person is born with. Enthusiasm is a characteristic available to anyone. How do you become enthusiastic? Simple. Become enthusiastic!
2. You can develop your positive self-image by developing your enthusiasm for yourself, other people, and life. By developing this enthusiasm, you become more positive towards life and, as a result, you become more popular and a more rewarding person to be near.
3. Get high on other people. Be easy to be with and give people that "around the fireplace," relaxed feeling.
4. See what's right with yourself. Do an asset analysis of yourself every day.
5. As you look at the history of humankind, it was always the enthusiastic, hopeful people who made the difference. Make the positive difference wherever you go and spread the contagion of enthusiasm.
6. Take your creative ideas via the Enthusiastic Expressway—the shortest route to Success City!

Keep your hot streak going. Continue to build your positive self-image by applying your formula of Creative Thinking (CT) and Enthusiasm (E) to your goals (G) to give them the lifting power they need to take you to SUCCESS CITY.

CHAPTER V

Letting the Power of Your Goals Give You a Lift

For millions of years, Mount Everest, the highest peak on earth towering majestically overhead at 29,028 feet, stood as an unconquerable goal and as the ultimate symbol of the human challenge. Over a quarter of a century ago, this snowcapped, 5½-mile-high piece of natural architecture lost its claim to fame. Thanks to Sir Edmund Hillary and Lenzing Norgay, Mount Everest is no longer man's highest reach to the heavens. On May 29, 1953, these two courageous men reached the summit once thought to be unattainable. In conquering Everest, Hillary and Norgay not only accomplished what was thought impossible, they clearly illustrated the infinity and superiority of man's capabilities. Everest now must look up to mankind.

Dramatic accomplishments such as the dangerous vertical trek to the top of Everest, the rapid advancement of technology, and the feasibility of shuttle service to various points in space attest to the fact that any human goal is achievable. And, although achievements in these areas of endeavor may lie beyond your realm of interest, the processes you use to accomplish your own goals are really the same as that used by the climbers, the technologists, and the designers of space travel.

Four of these processes have been explained in the preceding chapters. Just to remind ourselves once again, let us review them:

1. You recognize the power of self-image on success.
2. You take on the challenge of building your self-image to be a success-thinker.

3. You start your self-image building program by seeing a need or a dream and, through creative thinking, explore the possible ways of achieving that dream.
4. You keep your winning streak going by unleashing your enthusiasm to provide the mental power you need to achieve your goals.

Now give your unlimited creative potential and your enthusiastic zest for achievement the ultimate gift . . . a goal! Creativity and enthusiasm, like an arrow, need a target or else all of the efforts are wasted. Continue your journey to Success City by finding out where Success City is. With a map, you can see the destination and can avoid many backroads and detours. LOCK YOUR GOALS FIRMLY IN MIND AND GO FOR THEM. Then experience the enormous lifting power of your goals, because once you establish a goal firmly in your mind, it lifts you by finding the ways and means to achieve it.

THE GOAL MAKES THE DIFFERENCE

Think about the following everyday examples of how the power of goal setting works:

A salesperson wants to advance in his or her company and establishes the goal of winning over the big account.

A group of parents, concerned about the safety of their children, gets together and establishes a goal of having a traffic light installed near the neighborhood school.

A person sees a need for a delicatessen in the community and sets up a goal of opening the business.

An executive in charge of quality control aims at a goal of 95% flawless product.

A teen-age boy establishes a plan to win over the tall, svelte brunette in his class.

A high school student on the verge of failure establishes a goal of passing the final exams.

Yes, in each of these cases and in every day of your life, the same processes of goal achievement that the mountain climbers used is employed to bring about success, and in each of these cases, success began as a firm goal. What would happen if these people did not take a few moments to set goals? Imagine if the salesperson did not take some time to lock the goal of winning the big account firmly in mind. Most likely, the salesperson could never win over the big account. No goal—no lifting power. Imagine if the group of parents did not formally get together to set up the goal of having the traffic light installed in the neighborhood intersection. A traffic light would probably never be installed and the intersection would remain just as dangerous. No goal—no lifting power. Imagine if the person did not establish a goal to fill the need for a deli in the small community. There would not be a deli until someone else set up the goal. No goal locked firmly in mind—no lifting power. It's that simple.

And so it is with you. When you wander aimlessly and fail to lock your goals firmly in mind, no success is possible. Your goal, locked firmly in mind, makes a difference. Feed off the powerful lift that goal-setting gives you. The climbers who surmounted Everest or the salesperson determined to win the account had goals that gave them extra help. Their goals, like a magnet, attracted all of their actions.

HOW DO GOALS MAKE THE DIFFERENCE
AND GIVE LIFTING POWER?

Consciously establishing your goals gives you at least three advantages over a person who wanders aimlessly. First, a goal subconsciously lifts you by forcing you, even in your sleep, to find ways to achieve it. You perhaps have experienced having a determined goal of obtaining a new car, of buying a nifty new suit, of seeking admission to college, or of securing a new job. Did you find that your creativity found the way to achieve the goal? Besides helping your creativity to work for you, a firmly locked-in goal gives you a lift in another way. It gives you additional enthusiasm. Enthusiasm is the power and the energy to get your creative ideas ignited into potential action. Many an underdog football team won over a bigger, stronger opponent because its goal of victory was more firmly locked in. And when the goal was lifting them, they had more energy, more "psyche," more soul to make it happen. A third way that a firmly locked-in goal lifts you is by giving you direction when you are confused or lost. Goals again cite where you are in relation to your destination of Success City.

NEED A LIFT?

Try an experiment to test the lifting power of firmly locked-in goals. Ask yourself this question: What city, resort, vacation spot in the whole world would I like to visit within the next few years? Dream. Don't be shy. Would it be Hawaii, the pyramids of Egypt, the Orient, the Holy Land, the Rockies, the Grand Ole Opry in Nashville, Rio? Allow your mind to flow freely.

In my Think Your Way to Success Seminars, I encourage people to realize that their dream vacations are as inevitable as gravity if they firmly lock their destinations in their minds. I found in these seminars that if a person becomes fully determined to achieve that goal, it will be reached in every case, barring physical limitation. Even participants who told me later that they did not follow through with their original choice for a vacation spot, informed me that they chose another vacation spot in the interim or decided to achieve another goal instead. But none—that's right, none—of the goal setters ever told us that the goal could not have been reached. Your vacation goal, or any other goal, can be achieved, too, if you lock it firmly in mind.

Why could these locked-in goals be achieved in almost every case? First, you receive a lift from your creativity which will help you to find a way. Next, you start to visualize yourself achieving the goal, which gives you a lift. Then you fire up your enthusiasm and act on your plan, moving towards your destination. Finally, you become goal- or destination-centered and thus overcome every barrier along the way. Success! All because you locked a goal firmly in your mind. Don't lose the lift by floundering aimlessly about. After setting a goal, move towards it unhindered by avoiding the four traps on the road to Success City.

AVOIDING THE FOUR TRAPS ON THE ROAD TO YOUR GOALS

TRAP 1: F—Focusing on your ego instead of your goals.
TRAP 2: A—Accusing the world, other people, or yourself.
TRAP 3: I —Ignoring reality.
TRAP 4: L —Lacking goals to give you a lift.

AVOIDING THE FIRST TRAP ON THE ROAD TO YOUR GOALS: FOCUSING ON YOUR EGO INSTEAD OF YOUR GOALS

One surefire way to guarantee failure for yourself is to be more concerned with your ego than your goal. This problem is characteristic of what I call an EGO THINKER. An ego thinker spends all of his or her energies trying to look good or to save face with other people. The ego thinker loses sight of the war and concentrates on only one battle, "The Battle of the Ego!" Ego thinkers have lower self-images and are constantly worried about how they look to other people. They view every experience as a potential threat to their egos.

In my book *Turning People On* (1977), I contrast the styles of the ego thinker with the goal thinker. Observe closely the two different personalities and become determined not to get caught in the first failure trap—EGO!

The Ego Thinker Believes

"My ideas must always be the ones that people use. If someone gives a suggestion other than mine, it is an attack on my worthiness. And my ego couldn't handle someone disagreeing with me. So I must stubbornly fight to the bitter end, even by threatening to quit, if my ideas aren't the ones that are used. I must never be proven wrong."

but

The Goal Thinker Concludes

"It really doesn't matter whose ideas are used and who gets the credit for the ideas. The most important thing is that the BEST ideas are used. I want to hear the different ideas of everyone and then decide on the most effective course of action."

It's the simplest rule of psychology: Only the person who feels threatened is the one who needs to defend. The person with a poor self-image is the one who needs to defend his or her ego. The more positive an individual's self-image is, the more the person focuses in on the long-term goal and is less distracted with the issue of looking good or winning just to save face.

I saw the best example of how an ego thinker functions while serving as director of admissions and registrar of a Pennsylvania community college. The college administration established a goal of increasing its student enrollment. To meet this goal, one of my plans was to enlist the ideas of the students themselves on how they thought the best way of promoting the college might be. I selected a social psychology class. The project I gave them was entitled, "Applying the Principles of Social Psychology to Increase Student Enrollment." Put yourself in the excited students' shoes. Your very ideas could play a role in achieving a goal for your college.

My previous ideas about marketing a college were insignificant compared to the ideas that the students generated. I was so elated with their practical suggestions that I invited the dean of the school to listen to the ideas of these "turned on" students. An error in judgment on my part, to say the least! The ego thinking dean listened to the first inspired student who suggested that we form a speaker's bureau. The student explained that the speaker's bureau could be composed of students who would go to parent-teacher meetings and to civic, social, and business groups to discuss the program that the college offered. With arms folded in a closed fashion, the dean responded, "It'll never work. I've tried that before. You just can't get your foot in the door of these groups. Those people are looking for exciting speakers who have something to offer." The chin of the student who gave the suggestion dropped from noon to six o'clock. Put yourself in this student's shoes. You worked hard to make a contribution to achieve a goal, and you were told your idea wouldn't work.

Another student exclaimed, "Then why not invite a famous speaker, someone who has something to offer, to our college and open the lecture to the public? We could have an important political figure, writer, comedian, or even singer perform here. We could advertise in the newspapers, and when people come to the program, we could pass out literature about the school." The ego thinking dean rebuffed the idea by concluding that the college couldn't afford her idea because of the limited budget.

The dean was threatened. Like an ego thinker, the dean thought that if the student developed the idea instead of he himself on how to increase enrollment, it made him worth less and unneeded. When you put yourself in this student's shoes, how would you feel?

Have some fun with this one. Tap your understandings of how to motivate people and their ideas. Imagine that you are the dean of that school. Instead of being an ego thinker, use the ideas of Creative Thinking in Chapter III and the ideas of Enthusiasm (particularly for the suggestions of others) in Chapter IV. Watch how you could take suggestions like those given by the two students, expand on their ideas, and reach the goal of increased enrollment. Be a GOAL THINKER.

Consider the suggestion of the first student: "We could form a speaker's bureau composed of our own students and go out into the community to speak to a variety of groups about the programs our college offers." Now, with a totally open, GOAL THINKING approach, take just two minutes to expand on that student's idea. But remember, don't get ego involved. Put up red lights to your ego and green lights to your goal. Dream of the possible. Give the student credit and build on the idea.

What did you come up with in two minutes? If you came up with just one idea, you would be more effective in reaching the goal than a $30,000-a-year dean. And you've probably never even been a dean! Success through GOAL THINKING.

Here is another way that the ego thinker differs from the GOAL THINKER.

The Ego Thinker Believes:

"If I am criticized, it is a shot at my worth and I must immediately defend myself. I must continually make excuses when criticized or blame some-one else. Or, if I must, I'll attack some of my critic's own shortcomings."

but

The Goal Thinker Concludes:

"I am a fallible human being who is always looking to improve. When someone is kind enough to take the time to show me how to improve, I will seriously consider that person's suggestion. If it is relevant, great. If not, then I need not use it. But, unless I get new ideas, I really can't improve myself."

An Atlanta, Georgia advertising executive told me how he instructed his personnel department to hire new employees. In conjunction with other criteria, he instructed his staff to make sure that they hire people who are eager to want to improve. "How else can you learn and develop unless you are open to ideas and suggestions from others on ways of improving your style?" he shared with me. "I have our interviewers look at the applicant's weakest point and spend a good portion of the session discussing this deficiency with the applicant. We are not interested in how weak the point is, but we surely are interested in how the applicant responds to the criticism. For example, if the applicant were dismissed from a previous position, we, of course, do take that into consideration. But that dismissal in itself will not keep us from hiring the applicant. However, if, when confronted about the dismissal, the applicant begins to blame the previous employer, gives apologies, or makes excuses, this tells us that defensiveness is part of the person's style. And our advertis-ing firm has no room for defensive, apologetic people who waste time alibiing."

Again, the only people who have to be defensive are those who feel that their ego, their worth, is being attacked. The GOAL THINKER wants to improve, views criticism as assistance, and judges whether or not the criticism can be used to improve his or her lifestyle. Another way in which the ego thinker fools himself or herself and differs from the GOAL THINKER is in the person's view of competition.

The Ego Thinker Believes:

"If I'm defeated or if the competition beats me, I must put the opponent down and show how it was luck, dirty playing, or some other reason why this result occurred."

but

The Goal Thinker Concludes:

"If I am defeated, I lost. I'll congratulate the opponent, analyze the defeat, and make the corrections that I will need to increase the likelihood of my victory next time. With my new information, I'll be back, and I'm going to come on stronger than ever!"

The style of a true GOAL THINKER is unequivocally demonstrated in one of the most interesting stories I have ever heard. In a flight from South Bend to Chicago, I had the opportunity to sit with Mike Smith, the president of the Sugar Bowl Football Classic. Being interested in the thinking styles of successful athletes, it gave me a chance to learn more about the personalities of the best college football players in the world. So I asked the president of the New Year's Day pigskin attraction to share a little of his insight about the outstanding athletes he had met. With a big smile, the southerner, who commanded respect by his mere presence, said, "The truly great athletes are those who do not have to brag. They can accept losing without blaming or making excuses." Mr. Smith went on, "Let me share one of the most touching experiences I ever had with this kind of true athlete. Each year, one of my responsibilities is presenting the Sugar Bowl Outstanding Player of the Game Award to its outstanding player. A few years back, after the game one of the outstanding performers, Tony Dorsett, was misinformed that he had been selected to receive the coveted trophy. It was my responsibility to break the news to him that, in fact, someone else instead was voted the most valuable player. In the hectic pace with the national TV viewers anxiously waiting for the presentation, I informed Tony that someone else was to receive the award." Stop for a second and feel the entrance of this news in your life. How might you feel? Mr. Smith went on, "Well, after a brief pause, Tony looked at me and with a smile asked, 'Then can I stay and be one of the first people to congratulate the winner?'" What class! Imagine how an ego thinker would have responded to the same situation.

In contrast to Tony Dorsett's GOAL THINKING was an ego thinking style that one of my clients demonstrated towards competition. The dishevelled, yet attractive 21-year-old woman told me during one of our sessions that her boyfriend was seeing another girl. Phyllis whined, "And I keep telling him how ugly she is and that she has nothing going for her,"

I replied, "That's interesting—I mean, your telling him that this girl he sees is ugly. I personally think that I would do just the opposite. I'd pick out all of her positive points and tell him about all of the great things about her."

Startled, Phyllis looked at me in consternation and exclaimed, "Are you losing your mind? You want me to tell Tim about Jennifer's positive points? Why should I do something as stupid as that?"

"Simple," I responded. "There are two major ways of beating your competition. The petty and, in the long haul, ineffective way is to put your competition down. Just take a few seconds to think about how you view people who are always putting other people down."

After a pensive moment, the lackluster young lady answered, "Well, I guess I sort of lose respect for them. It gets sickening after a while, and I don't enjoy being with them. I'd rather be with someone positi . . ." In midsentence, the petite blonde stopped. After a delay, she replied, "Oh, maybe I'm losing Tim because I'm always downing Jennifer. Perhaps I'm becoming sickening to be around. But," she went on to say, "if I am positive and tell Tim about her good points, won't he then become more attracted to her?"

"Well, that, too, is up to you." I went on, "You see, Phyllis, I said that there are two possible ways to beat your competition. The first way is to put the opponent down. That is what we call an ego thinker's style. But the other way to win is to pick yourself up. Start by praising the good points of your competition. This, in itself, picks you up because it shows people that you have so much self-confidence that you don't have to be a pint-sized thinker, even about your competition. Next, you pick yourself up by becoming a GOAL THINKER. You tell me that your goal is to win Tim over. So take all of the efforts you now use to down Jennifer and energetically fire up your enthusiasm and become a new, exciting, beautiful, refreshing person. Let's look at all of the things that you could do to achieve that goal. First, you could wear your hair a different way each time you are with Tim. Then you could spend a little more time with your clothing, makeup, and, yes, working on your smile. You could then think about Tim's life and his work and get interested and enthusiastic about him. You could read new, exciting books, develop new ideas, become a more interesting and even a more positive person. You are only limited by your thinking. Rise up; get better; share his dream and yours. Win Tim over by thinking in tons, not pints.

"So, Phyllis, it's up to you! You decide which would be more gratifying to you—losing to someone you feel is ugly or winning over competition you feel is fantastic?"

Be a GOAL THINKER. Take advantage of the lifting power of your goals.

FIVE WAYS TO BE A GOAL THINKER

1. Make your goals more important than your ego.

2. Give credit to anyone who gives you an idea. Remember, it doesn't matter whose idea it is. The important thing is to decide which idea will be most effective in helping you to reach your goal.

3. Be a "criticism welcomer." People pay for advice and suggestions every day. You can receive free help through criticism. Remember, ultimately you have the power to choose whether the criticism has merit and whether or not you will use it. But, at least, criticism gives you an option to think about what you didn't have before.

4. "Make defeat sweet." Turn defeats into victories, not by blaming or excusing (ego thinking), but by analyzing what went wrong. Correct the error and move rapidly toward the goal (GOAL THINKING).

5. Elevate your competition! Share the genuine assets of your competitors with people. It gives you credibility and demonstrates your self-confidence in yourself and your product. Be a class act, like Tony Dorsett.

On the road to your goals, avoid the first of the four failure traps—that of focusing on your ego. When you become a GOAL THINKER, you are lifted by the goal, allowing you to move full speed ahead in your journey to Success City. Now, overcome the second failure trap of accusing or blaming other people, life, or yourself.

AVOIDING THE SECOND FAILURE TRAP ON THE ROAD TO YOUR GOALS: ACCUSING OTHER PEOPLE, LIFE, OR YOURSELF

Observe the following dialogue about two different styles of dealing with a problem. Contrast the reactions of the ACCUSATION THINKER with the reactions of the RESPONSIBLE, GOAL-ORIENTED THINKER. The incident begins when both people discover that the driver's car ran out of gas on the way to a dinner party.

Passenger: I don't believe it. How stupid of you. (ACCUSATION THINK-
             ING.) When is the last time you bought gas?

Driver: Does it matter?

Passenger: You are so irresponsible. (ACCUSATION THINKING.) Now
             we'll be late, for sure. Everyone's dinner will be held up because
             you, you ninny, didn't plan ahead. How many miles does this
             piece of junk get per gallon anyway?

Driver: Does it matter right now?

Passenger: Don't get so smart when I try to talk to you. And to top it all, of all
             places you pick to run out of gas, you pick a place that is miles
             from a gas station. At least, if you were going to run out, you
             could have run out in the city. This is unbelievable. If I catch a
             cold in this freezing car, it's all your fault. (ACCUSATION
             THINKING.)

Driver: The car won't run until I get gas. I'm going to get gas now.
             (RESPONSIBLE, GOAL-ORIENTED THINKING.)

Do you know both parties in this dialogue? Of course, the ACCUSATION
THINKER gets nowhere and is obsessed with finding the blame rather
than the solution.

As a frequent traveller, I have the opportunity to observe ACCUSA-
TION THINKERS in action. I recall one particular incident a few years
ago while delayed at O'Hare Airport in Chicago because of excessive
rain, wind, and cloudy conditions. I listened to scores of ACCUSATION
THINKERS blame the world, life, and airport personnel. But I decided to
make my wait a productive one. While looking out at the rain from the
Ambassador Lounge, I wrote the following poem:

> Days and days of sloppy rain
> Led the ACCUSATION THINKER to complain;
> But the other guy, the GOAL THINKING fella,
> Looked at the rain and created the umbrella.

The accuser, like the passenger in the gasless car or the cynic looking at
the rain, spends valuable energies digging up the source of blame for the
situation. There are tremendous short-term advantages to this style.
After all, if you can track down the blame for why you have not made it
from third base to home plate, you can sit back, get angry, and creatively
cultivate unlimited reasons why you didn't succeed. In my book, *You Can
Do It: How to Encourage Yourself,* I've listed some of the main sources of

blame and some of the blame receivers. Learn to recognize these defense mechanisms when they try to cloud your success thinking.

ACCUSING OR BLAMING STYLES

1. *Group Blame,* e.g., the Russians, the Americans, society in general, the referees, the Beatles, the Supreme Court, etc., etc. Of course, you could go on if you really wanted to get into ACCUSATION THINKING. Be a RESPONSIBLE, GOAL-ORIENTED THINKER and constantly conclude, "It doesn't matter who did what to me. Where am I now and what is my next goal? What is my next logical step towards this goal? Let me get started." Let the archeologists dig up the past. Be a GOAL-ORIENTED inventor and create the future.

2. *Other person blame.* "You made me . . . angry, sick, fail, feel inferior, lose, hit you, late, look like a fool, fat by the way you fed me, starve because you didn't feed me lunch, miss my dentist's appointment because you forgot to remind me, etc." Again, a creative ACCUSATION THINKER could go on and on by always finding another person to blame for not succeeding. But where do these accusations lead you? Nowhere. A truly RESPONSIBLE, GOAL-ORIENTED THINKER takes the same circumstances and concludes, "Other people can't make me angry or late or fat. While other people can act the way they want to, it's up to me to choose how I choose to react to them." (See Chapter VII, Rational Thinking.) "When I am angry, it is because I choose to become angry at what someone else said or how someone else acted. While I'm not in charge of this other person's actions, I am in charge of my reaction to what happened. That's how powerful I am when I am GOAL ORIENTED."

3. *Thing Blame.* "This weather makes me miserable." "This traffic jam makes me angry." "If it wouldn't be for this putter, I could have golfed par today." "This inferiority complex of mine keeps me from meeting people." Remember, the RESPONSIBLE, GOAL-ORIENTED THINKER realizes, "It's not the economy that has me fuming, but it is how I choose to react to the economy that makes me boil. And I am in charge of my reaction to the economy, so I will develop a plan to deal with the financial situation."

4. *Self-blame.* "I'm too stupid." "I'm not the kind of person who can . . . resist snacks, get along with people, stay on a task." The self-accuser differs from the RESPONSIBLE, GOAL-ORIENTED THINKER in that the self-accuser sees a personal weakness and then gives up. The responsible, goal-thinking person sees the same weakness and decides to do something about it and then moves on to achieve the goal.

A good example I experienced that demonstrated the difference between the self-blamer and the responsible person occurred while I observed two fifth-grade students analyze why they failed a test.

Jimmy: (SELF-ACCUSING) I'm stupid. I hate tests. I'm never taking any of these tests again. I'm worthless because I failed.

Charlie: (RESPONSIBLE, GOAL-ORIENTED reaction to the same failure) Jimmy, you think you failed the test because you're worthless. Do you know why I failed the test? I didn't fail the test because I was worthless. The reason I failed the test was because I didn't put the right answers in the right places. I guess I'll have to study next time so I can get the right answers.

Which style, Jimmy's self-accusing or Charlie's responsible, goal-oriented style, is more likely to lead to future success? I believe the latter. People who are humble and get down on themselves deserve their humility.

These styles of accusing or blaming are increasingly being recognized as the source of most human failure and unhappiness. The innovative psychologists, Albert Ellis and Robert Harper, write about blame in *A New Guide to Rational Living* (Ellis and Harper, 1974, p. 113):

We can designate the essence of emotional disturbance in a single word: BLAMING. If you would stop, really stop blaming yourself, others or unkind fate, you would virtually find it impossible to feel emotionally upset about anything. And you can probably omit "virtually" from the preceding sentence.

FOUR WAYS TO THINK YOUR WAY TO SUCCESS AND BE A RESPONSIBLE GOAL-ORIENTED THINKER

1. *Act, don't catastrophize.* For example, when your car runs out of gas, don't ask why or accuse life. Instead, get gas and move on to your destination. When your boss tells you that you will lose your sales position in six months unless you increase sales, make a plan. Take a sales course, make every appointment you schedule, work triple hard. Become the successful salesperson your boss has never seen. Your new thoughts and views will make the difference in your success. Contrast that success style with the catastrophizing, blaming style.

2. *Take charge of all of the power you have within you by the way you look at things.* Regardless of how challenging circumstances might be,

don't spend your time accusing. Spend your time dealing with the problem, taking responsibility, setting new winning goals, and moving toward those goals.

3. *Get on course.* An airplane doesn't travel in a perfect line from one city to another. It makes a series of calculations and adjustments along the way. When it gets off course, it simply gets back on course. It's the same way with you and your goals. Get to your destination by following the similar success pattern. When you get off course (failure, rejection, mistakes), don't become an EGO THINKER and give up. Instead, become a DESTINATION THINKER and simply get back on course. Your goal is awaiting your arrival.

4. *Imbed these few words of wisdom in your heart and you will reach home plate every time.* The four maxims are: "How I got to where I am today is irrelevant. The past is past. But where I go tomorrow is up to me. Yes, IT'S UP TO ME TO DEVELOP A GOAL AND TAKE ADVANTAGE OF THE LIFTING POWER OF THE GOAL."

Now *Think Your Way to Success* by avoiding the third failure trap—ignoring reality.

AVOIDING THE THIRD FAILURE TRAP ON THE ROAD TO YOUR GOALS: IGNORING REALITY

I believe that life is incredibly simple and that it is people who make it complex. Most people frustrate themselves and make their lives difficult by making THE ULTIMATE HUMAN MISTAKE—the mistake of losing sight of reality. 99% of us are partially out of touch with reality at one time or another. At those moments when we refuse to accept reality, we find ourselves "two degrees off plumb." These are the times when we confuse "what we wish to be" with "what actually is" in life. We reduce ourselves to having the intelligence of a dog chasing the wheels of a car. Instead, succeed by saving yourself a lot of energy by chiseling these three words into your mental fabric: "WHAT IS, IS."*

Motivation lectures and positive attitude books often neglect an important point about reality. Your start toward Success City is reality. If you are so high that you think you could fly, it would be a grave error to ignore the reality of the law of gravity. As Bertrand Russell once commented, "Any man who maintains that happiness comes wholly from within should be

---

*These words were so meaningful to a barber, Jeffrey Paul, that after I used them in a Pittsburgh, Pennsylvania seminar, he sent me a shirt with the words, "WHAT IS, IS," on it. I wear it when I need to be reminded to accept a fact of reality.

prepared to spend thirty-six hours in rags in a blizzard without food." This point is not meant to discourage you. I feel, perhaps, a parental need not to have you fall flat on your face. That will only discourage you and keep you from being successful, thus not helping the rest of humanity. We need you. So face the fact that there will be barriers, but through creative thinking, enthusiasm, and goal setting, these obstacles can be overcome. So when I say, "WHAT IS, IS," it is meant to encourage you. When you accept this fact of reality, you have an invigorating, challenging starting point. Dreamers who faced reality and learned how to reach the heavens despite the realities of gravity were those who designed planes and spacecraft. Wishers, on the other hand, who didn't take reality into consideration only experienced frustration. *THINK YOUR WAY TO SUCCESS* by getting a keen sense of reality. Never again be frustrated by putting reality "where it isn't."

THINKING YOUR WAY TO SUCCESS BY SEEING REALITY FOR WHAT IT IS

Lock into your mind forever these three facts about reality, and you will find yourself managing your life by a realistic goal orientation:

FACT 1: Reality is not what we wish it to be; rather, reality is what it is.

FACT 2: Reality is not interested in what each of us thinks it "should be;" rather, reality is what it is.

FACT 3: Reality is not just or fair; rather, reality is what it is.

FACT 1: Reality is not what we wish it to be; rather, reality is what it is.

Don't get caught in the "wisher's web." Reality has no respect for wishers. Wishing away a thunderstorm or wishing a million-dollar-lottery win are the almost guaranteed routes of failures. Not only is wishing an ineffective course of action, but it is a frustrating route as well. That is what concerns me about you. I don't want you to be discouraged in your trip to Success City because you made the error of wishing that the 200-mile journey was only 50 miles and eventually became frustrated. It is 200 miles. But after facing reality head on, if you use creative thinking and enthusiasm, you will find a way. People living on the Sea of Fantasy off of the Coast of Reality dream up a world that doesn't exist, and then they get frustrated when the world they wished for "lets them down." The world, in fact, didn't let them down. The problem was that they were living on wishes which were a false "pick-me-up" in the first place. If you want to eat, stop wishing and start fishing. Don't compromise one moment of your dream; just make sure that you are clear that your starting point is on firm ground.

FACT 2: Reality is not interested in what each of us thinks it "should be;" rather, reality is what it is.

Most of the people in the world bat their heads up against the wall of reality by confusing what they think "should be" with what actually is. If you take the following sentence and make it part of your life, you will never again be unhappy or frustrated for more than just a few seconds. Here it is: THERE ARE NO SHOULDS, OUGHTS, OR MUSTS IN THE WHOLE WORLD . . . NONE! EVERY TIME WE SAY ANY OF THOSE WORDS, WE ARE RUNNING FULL FORCE AWAY FROM REALITY. INSTEAD OF SAYING "SHOULD," "OUGHT," OR "MUST," LEARN THE ONLY WORDS THAT WILL LEAD TO SUCCESS. What are those magic words? They are: WHAT IS MY PLAN? Observe how people sit in their SHOULD seats and run away from reality. Allow me to share a few of my experiences with SHOULD THINKERS.

A client of mine who came late for one of our appointments told me apologetically, "I'm sorry I'm late, but I caught ten red lights in a row. You SHOULD never get that many." My response was the only logical one I could give. I asked Barb, "Exactly how many red lights in a row SHOULD you get?" Think about it.

While speaking at a teachers' convention in Edmonton, Alberta, one of the bellhops at the hotel apologized to me for the freezing weather. The kind man said, "It really SHOULDN'T be this cold here at this time of the year." I responded again in the only logical way I knew. I asked, "How cold SHOULD it be?" He had, believe it or not, an answer. He knocked my socks off by responding, "It should be about ten degrees warmer." Although I was taken back by his response, I wasn't finished with his comment that "it SHOULD be about ten degrees warmer." I asked, "WHAT'S YOUR PLAN?"

A fellow professor with whom I shared an office was angrily hovering over his desk one day demanding, "I left my car keys on the desk. They SHOULD be there!" Looking at the empty desk, I retorted, "But they're not." While pointing accusingly to his desk, he came back with, "But they SHOULD be." "But they're not," I said again. "But they SHOULD be," he growled. I informed the professor that he had at least two options. I said, "It seems to me that the keys, whether they SHOULD or SHOULD NOT be on your desk, are, in fact, not on your desk. Believe me, there is a greater chance that your keys are in Rio than there is of them being here on this desk. There are at least one or two things you could do. You could, for the rest of your life, stand by this desk and say, 'The keys SHOULD be here, they SHOULD be here,' or secondly, you could look elsewhere. Which decision would help you to find your keys?"

Another beautiful friend of mine, who was usually quite in touch with reality, had one weak moment. Quite annoyed, Carol said to me, "My oil burner broke down and it SHOULDN'T. It was just checked, and I even have a warranty." I asked, "Did you show the oil burner the warranty?" I went on to add, "For the rest of your life, you can stand by the oil burner, chanting, 'You SHOULD work, you SHOULD work, because I have a warranty,' or you could call to get it fixed. Take just a few minutes to think the matter through. Which do you think would be a more productive course of action?"

Finally, I won't leave this topic on reality until I relate this incredible experience. While out on a date, the woman I was with shared with me the great news that she began her new diet that morning. I was elated for her goal-setting spirit. Soon afterward, we arrived at a birthday party. It wasn't long before the hostess was walking with her tray, serving cake and ice cream. When the bright-eyed woman turned to us, she enticed my friend, who had just claimed she started her diet that day, by asking, "Would you care for some marble cake and ice cream?" Hold on to your sombrero when you hear, in this chapter on reality, my friend's response. "Oh, I SHOULDN'T have any . . . but I guess it won't hurt!" I looked at her and responded, "What would be your second guess?" Yes, LIFE IS INCREDIBLY SIMPLE, but people make it difficult when they do as psychologist Albert Ellis says, "They SHOULD on themselves."

Eliminate the words "should," "ought," and "must" and instead say, "WHAT IS MY PLAN?" You will be amazed how easy it is to be successful. You will also be amazed with how many people who fail have vocabularies filled with those unproductive words. THINK YOUR WAY TO SUCCESS by becoming a "WHAT'S-MY-PLAN?" thinker.

FACT 3: Reality is not just or fair; rather, reality is what it is.

It would do my mind and heart a lot of good if I didn't have to write this because it is inconsistent with my former strongly held beliefs. But it appears to me that if you want to succeed and help the world, you need to accept the fact that REALITY IS NEITHER JUST NOR FAIR. The minute that we allow this insight to permeate our minds, that's the minute that we can bring about positive change. Observe Kathy, who's caught in the unfairness trap:

Kathy: It just isn't fair. Carolyn can eat all of the pastry that she wants, and she never gains a pound. Yet, if I so much as look at cakes or cookies, I put on weight.

Where does Kathy take her complaint? Right, there is nowhere to go! Kathy is producing her own frustration because she believes that reality is not fair to her. Her frustration, remember, is not due to the fact that she gains weight, but is related to her unwillingness to accept reality the way it "is." Imagine if Kathy accepted the fact that she gains weight easily and used all of her energies to plan a diet, instead of using her energies to complain. We ask Kathy, "Who said things are fair? Why must they be fair?" Obviously, Kathy is destined to a life of frustration because she does not accept an element of the world that she believes does not work in her favor.

We might mention to Kathy, "Yes, it is unfair. But maybe, if you think of it, the unfairness of life has actually worked in your favor. For example, you have a healthy heart, you eat three meals a day, you have the ability to read, you have two TV's, and most of the people in the world would enthusiastically change place with you at this moment today. Yes, true, the world is unfair, but look to what you have and develop a plan to help other people.

It is important for me to say here that justice is a most noteworthy ideal and that I would be glad to be right up front leading the parade for a more just world. But the fact is that the world is not just or fair, and demanding that it be so is not only ineffective, but frustrating. Together, let's develop a plan to change that fact.

Now, avoid the fourth failure trap, which is the failure to establish goals.

AVOIDING THE FOURTH FAILURE TRAP ON THE WAY TO YOUR GOALS: LACKING GOALS TO GIVE YOURSELF A LIFT

Cheshire Cat: What's the matter, little girl? May I help you?

Alice: I'm lost. I don't know which road to take.

Cheshire Cat: Well, where is it that you would like to go?

Alice: I don't know.

Cheshire Cat: Well, if you don't know where you'd like to go, it doesn't much matter which road you take.

(Paraphrased from *Alice in Wonderland*)

Alice did not have a goal to lift her. She was wandering aimlessly; she was lost. Even if she had a map, it wouldn't have made a difference since she had no destination. If she were destined to go any place, she was destined for no place. Observe how successes differ from failures in the way people talk about their goals for the day.

Failures	*Successes*
"I SHOULD get the car washed to-day." (Tentative goal not firmly locked in mind, and consequently has no lifting power.)	"I'm definitely getting my car washed in the Washarama at ten o'clock." (Goal firmly locked in and consequently has lifting power.)
"Maybe someday I'll stop smoking. Smoking isn't the best thing for a person." (Very tentative.)	"I'm quitting smoking right now by not having a cigarette all day. Then tomorrow I'll do the same." (Firm goal.)

Who will most likely succeed—the person who takes advantage of his or her goals or the person who "shoulds" or "coulds" or "maybes" his or her way around the commitment to a firm goal?

When you firmly lock a goal in your mind, all of your feelings, thoughts, and actions begin to work for you to help you achieve your goal. Psychiatrists Alfred Adler, Rudolf Dreikurs, and Kurt Adler point out that "all behavior has a purpose or a goal." Either take charge of your goal or it takes charge of you. When you lock a goal firmly in mind, every one of your feelings, thoughts, and actions come under your subconscious control. When you fail to develop a firm goal, your unrealized goals take over.

In *You Can Do It: How to Encourage Yourself,* I introduce the concept of the unrealized goal:

Although you are the executive of all of your feelings, thoughts, and actions, most of the time you fail to make your goals clear. And when you fail to develop clear goals, other unrealized goals may take over. Remember that your feelings, thoughts, and actions are constantly being pulled by either your firm goals or your unrealized goals.

Unrealized goals are a talented and formidable opponent to you. Short-term satisfaction is one example of an unrealized goal that can snatch your employees (your feelings, thoughts, and actions) right from under you! Consider Ethel, whose firm goal is to lose weight. Observe the struggle between her unrealized goal and her firm goal as she is confronted with a high-calorie ice cream cake just after she has finished a big meal!

UNREALIZED GOAL	FIRM GOAL
I want this ice cream cake now.	I want to lose weight.

FEELINGS:
It makes me so angry. Why do I have to be so heavy? It just isn't fair. It's so depressing when I look in a mirror. Well, I'm so bad off, what more will a little ice cream cake hurt?

FEELINGS:
I feel so good that I can walk away from this ice cream cake. And if I think I feel good now, just think how good I'll feel if I lose those 10 pounds because of sacrifices like this.

THINKING:
It shouldn't be this hard to diet. Just this one time won't hurt.

THINKING:
It's difficult to turn this down, but I can stand it.

It's unfair. My sister can eat all she wants, and I just look at food, and I gain weight. Heck, I'm not going to deprive myself of this food.

My sister is fortunate, because she can eat all she wants. That has nothing to do with me, however.

I deserve this ice cream cake. Look how hard I worked all week.

I might deserve the cake. It would taste good for about five minutes. But then I have to live with its effects. It isn't worth it and directly interferes with my goals.

I'll start my diet tomorrow instead.

I have control now, and it won't be any easier tomorrow.

ACTIONS:
Ethel eats the ice cream cake, and the unrealized goal wins out.

ACTIONS:
Ethel walks away from the ice cream cake. The firm goal wins out.

Identify some unrealized goals in your past that have generally won the battle. Remember, you as a human being are so powerful that you decide the winner. Successful people are those who direct their feelings, thoughts, and actions toward their firm goals. They state their goal, know their resources, and mobilize their feelings, thoughts, and actions into the desired direction, and they defeat their unrealized goals.

. . . Courageous people take advantage of the constant pulling power of their positive goals.

(Losoncy, 1980, pp. 38-40)

DEVELOP FIRM GOALS AND BE THE CHIEF EXECUTIVE OF YOUR LIFE

If you feel that your thoughts, feelings, and actions have been out of your control, you have become your own worst enemy and a slave to your unrealized goals. You have chosen to be a pawn rather than the chief executive of your life. Rise up and overthrow your feelings of powerlessness. Put yourself where you belong—in charge of your life. You can do it right now by doing one simple thing. Write down and firmly lock in a destination for yourself. Then watch the unmatched power of your goals lift you to them like the top of Mt. Everest called the climbers!

1. Every time you establish a goal and lock it in as firmly as the Mt. Everest climbers locked their goal in, you give yourself lifting power. The more firmly the goal is locked in, the greater the lift.
2. *THINK YOUR WAY TO SUCCESS* by avoiding the four traps that FAILURE THINKERS get caught in:
   F—*F*ocusing on the ego rather than the goal
   A—*A*ccusing the world, other people, and/or yourself
   I —*I*gnoring reality
   L—*L*acking goals to give you lifting power
3. Let the power of your goals give you a lift to success by being a GOAL THINKER rather than an EGO THINKER. Make your goals more important than your ego. Give credit to anyone who gives you an idea, even when it differs from your own idea. Be a "criticism welcomer." Make defeat sweet by the powers of GOAL THINKING. And finally, build your self-image by "elevating your competition."
4. Let the power of your goals give you a lift to success by being a RESPONSI-BLE, GOAL-ORIENTED THINKER rather than an ACCUSATION THINKER. Spend your valuable life energies dealing with the obstacles, not tracking down a source of blame. When you get a flat tire, don't accuse life or the highway system. Fix the flat and move on. When you find yourself straying from a goal through failure, rejection, or mistakes, become a DES-TINATION, GOAL ORIENTED THINKER. Correct the mistakes and get back on course. Be a responsible person by sizing up any situation no matter how difficult, and saying, "It's up to me to develop a firm goal and take advantage of its lifting power."
5. Let the power of your goals give you a lift to success by realizing that "What is, is!" This powerful insight will help you overcome an entangled life in "wisher's web" or a traffic jam on the Fairness Freeway. Get off living on the Sea of Fantasy and move to the Coast of Reality by eliminating all "shoulds," "oughts," and "musts" from your vocabulary. Like all Successes do, say, "WHAT'S MY PLAN?" instead of saying SHOULD or SHOULDN'T.
6. Finally, let the power of your goals lift you to success by firmly locking in your goals. Be the chief executive of your life by taking charge of your goals and avoiding the powerless feeling of being ruled by your unrealized goal. You Can Do It!

You have come a long way to *Thinking Your Way to Success.* You have developed a positive self-image by using the unlimited powers of your creative thinking (CT); you have ignited your energy system of enthusiasm (E); you have propelled your ideas toward a firmly locked in

GOAL (G). How could you miss? Now make your path easier by designing a positive environment that will work for you:

$$CT + E + G + DPE + \ldots = SUCCESS$$
$$\text{(Designing}$$
$$\text{a Positive}$$
$$\text{Environment)}$$

CHAPTER VI

Designing a Positive Environment that Will Work for You

Congratulations! I have great news for you! You have just been hired to one of the most prestigious professional positions in the world. I am pleased to announce that today you begin your new post as Director of Environmental Engineering for the most important account in the world . . . your own.

Yes, today you take on the responsibility of designing your "Setting for Success." Please don't take this new position lightly. The stimulation or inspiration that your environment can give you is all extra help in your journey to Success City. Your environment helps to develop your unlimited number of creative thoughts (Chapter III). Your environment plays a role in igniting your enthusiasm (Chapter IV), and your environment can be a constant reminder for you to stay on the goal-centered track (Chapter V). Taking charge of your environment and making it work for you is one of the biggest lifts you can give yourself.

Just as the air you breathe in from your physical environment affects your physical health, your psychological environment affects your psychological health. When pollution levels are high, the negative contaminants you breathe in circulate throughout your body. When the negative thought pollution in your environment is high, it makes it difficult for you to be a creative, enthusiastic, goal-directed person.

Take charge today. Engineer a mass clean-up of your attitude environment by eliminating polluted thinking. Create a fresh, idea-inspiring, spring morning feeling in your surroundings. Then watch your creative ideas, powered by your enthusiasm, flow into successful actions.

YOUR ENVIRONMENT IS ALSO A PRODUCT OF YOU

Your environment is a powerful influence on you. In fact, the most popular school of psychological thought in the 1960's was Behavioral Psychology, usually credited to the brilliant B.F. Skinner. Behaviorists, as the advocates of Skinner's view were called, argued that people were a product of their environments. You could understand human behavior simply by understanding the person's environment. To change behavior, the behavioral engineer would simply alter the environment.

In the first chapter, I suggested that our environments "tend to" affect us in certain ways. An environment with an abundance of encouragement "tends to" invite positive behavior, while a negative environment "tends to" invite discouragement. I agreed that environment is important, but I rejected the idea that the person is totally and helplessly a product of environment. In fact, I believe that the opposite is even more true; that is, your environment is a PRODUCT OF YOU. This is powerful news. This view asserts that you are an active creator of your environment rather than just a passive marionette on the strings of the mentality of the people around you.

If you doubt that you play a role in creating your environment, the next time you go to a restaurant, give a warm smile to the waiter or waitress. Observe the reaction of the server to this positive approach. Now approach another server with a gruff "Where were you? I've been waiting for a long time!" Contrast the two responses you receive and see if the environmental reactions differ when you change your style.

Yes, you are Director of Environmental Engineering for the construction of a positive success setting for yourself. And the great news is that you have many, many people and unlimited natural resources to assist you in developing a winning environment. Your new environment can start and end on a positive note.

DESIGNING AN ENVIRONMENT TO WORK FOR YOU

8 Positive Strategies
P—*P*ut positive people in your environment.
O—*O*verlook small negatives in your environment.
S—*S*witch the big negatives into positives.
I —*I*nfluence positively the environments of other people.
T—*T*reasure what you already have as part of your life.
I —*I*ntellectually stimulate yourself by "Ideaing-Up" your environment.
V—*V*acation your mind and your senses in new environments.
E—*E*xpose yourself to positive media.

ENVIRONMENTAL ENGINEERING STRATEGY NO. 1: PUT POSITIVE PEOPLE IN YOUR ENVIRONMENT

Raise your ecological standards. No longer allow yourself to be a dumping site for rotten reasoning, noxious negativism, or poisonous perceptions. Stop feeding your thoughts on the failure fodder so plentiful in environmental dumping sites. Lower the pollution index in your environment as fast as the dog licks a dish.

The first step in the Environmental Engineering cleanup is to surround yourself with the most positive people you know. When you do, you'll become more creative, more enthusiastic, more goal-centered, and you'll even develop a more positive self-image. Negative people in your environment who constantly point out everything that's wrong with life make it easy for you to get down on living. And when you do this, you feel negative about yourself.

Most negative people can easily be recognized and quickly diagnosed. Engineer people out of your environment who use opening lines like:

"I shouldn't tell you what people are saying about you and your ideas, but . . ."

"Let me play the devil's advocate for a minute . . ."

"You never were very good at . . ."

I wouldn't waste my time with that idea of yours."

"You! You could never . . ."

Also stay away from people who have the bad, tragic doom news, or people who are worried about the sun running out of its energy in the next seven billion years.

When people focus on the negatives of life or on your negative behaviors, they are trying to lead you down Loser's Lane to show you where they live.

ISSUE THE WARNING TO THE WORLD OF NEGATIVE THINKERS: CEASE AND DESIST!

Negative people who try to bully themselves into your attitude ecology system need to be restrained. Tell them to cease and desist or you will have them arrested for first degree mindslaughter. Taking advice from negative failures is like hiring a bankrupt person to be your financial advisor. As Director of Environmental Engineering for yourself, you have the right and the obligation to remove toxic thinking. Your ulcers, migraines, hypertension, and depression may be related to being tensed, stressed, or influenced by negative thinkers. Clean up your thoughts and give a sensitive but stern warning to negative thinking people, like:

"I find that the last few times we were together, I walked away upset."

"I felt discouraged the other day when we talked, and I think that it would be best if we didn't talk when you are feeling negative. However, I'd love to get together again when you are feeling more positive."

A few comments said not aggressively (see Chapter IX for further discussion on being assertive), but firmly and fairly, will not only help you, but, in fact, help the negative person. Oftentimes, you will see your friend the next time with a big cheery positive smile.

Successful environmental engineering involves, first, putting negative people on probation, and, second, hiring positive consultants to help you design your success environment.

HIRE A BOARD OF POSITIVE CONSULTANTS TO HELP DESIGN YOUR ENVIRONMENT

Don't take on such an important challenge as designing your environment by yourself. As Director of Environmental Engineering, you have the power to not only dehire, but to hire people to assist you. So hire your own board of free advisors to be part of your supersuccessfully stimulating environment.

The simplest task in the world is selecting the people who will be on your board of positive consultants. Identify at least five people based on these qualifications: (1) You feel positive about yourself and life when you are with them; (2) you feel courageously willing to try new experiences and take new risks when you are with them; and (3) you feel free to speak and share even your craziest new ideas in their presence. Please take this important exercise to heart. Jot down the names of the people you have honored by your selections. In your environment, A POSITIVE FRIEND IS LIKE A RARE GEM.

When you have established whom you would like on your board of advisors, make a point of telling each of them that you have read a book on the importance of having positive consultants. Tell each of these people the three requirements for a person to be a positive advisor and that you have selected him or her for the position. Then ask each of the group to consider accepting a position on your advisory board and express your confidence in the fact that acceptance involves nothing more than continuing to be himself or herself. I'm sure your comments will elate all of them to no end. How would you feel if someone complimented you by saying that out of everyone he knew, you were one of the most positive influences on his or her life? After you share your news, you will rarely find any one of these people "down" in your presence.

Become determined to spend more time with each of your board members in the future. Make more plans to see them and talk with them, even if only on the telephone. When you consider the fact that people pay $60 to $125 an hour to talk with their psychiatrist or to listen to motivation lecturers, friends who help a person feel positive are worth quite a lot. Don't neglect positive advisors, the richest source of input.

And the great news is that even if you can't be near your board of advisors because of distance or timing, it doesn't matter. When facing a difficult decision or a challenging situation, recall your advisors' thinking by visualizing their reactions to the event. In your imagination, confront each positive person with the situation and picture each one's response and advice. You will find the results of their advice to be quite interesting, if not incredible. Most of your free advisors will probably agree on the best course of action for you! As Director of Environmental Engineering for yourself, hire the most positive people you know and watch your positive self-image grow. Now, add an honorary board of advisors composed of the most inspirational thinkers in the world.

APPOINT AN HONORARY BOARD OF ADVISORS FOR YOURSELF

Don't limit your advisory list to people that you know. Add to your list people whom you respect, even if you don't even know them personally. Allow me to share with you some of the people on my Honorary Board of Environmental Advisors. I have ten members, all of them successful people, and I provide balance by including both liberal and conservative advisors:

Lew Losoncy
Director of Environmental Engineering

Honorary Board of Advisors

Conservative Members	Liberal Members
Courageous Achievers	Creative Envisioners
Dr. Jonas Salk (found cure for the disease of polio)	The ant who moved the rubber tree plant in the song "High Hopes"

Terry Fox (see Chapter IV)

Irvin Westheimer (founder
of Big Brothers)

Orville and Wilbur Wright

Rose (from Chapter I)

The Little Engine That Could ("I
think I can, I think I can.")

Annie, from the play *Annie* ("The
Sun'll Come Out Tomorrow")

When I need advice, I consult with each of the members of the board and ask, "What would you do if you were faced with this challenge?" I have received some powerful and successful advice from these board members. Just imagine the combined advice you could receive from your Honorary Board and your regular Board of Advisors. Imagine how much more likely you will be to succeed than people who surround themselves with negative people.

On this note, allow me to share with you how I developed the idea of the Honorary Board and what it has done for me. As you may recall from Chapter I, I failed in not only some high school subjects, but some college courses as well. My greatest weaknesses were in vocabulary and grammar. But, in spite of these weaknesses, years later I decided to write a book. After two chapters of the manuscript were completed, I took it to my former college English professor and asked him if I should continue. The prof returned the manuscript a few days later and told me he didn't feel I could ever get a publisher and that I should give up the idea of writing a book. My determination went down like a sledge hammar falls. I gave up.

A few days later, I shared that experience and my discouragement with my students in a Psychology of Communications class. The students were deeply touched—their prof, usually positive, was giving up! At our next class meeting, my students brought me two gifts: a rubber tree plant, and a record of the song "High Hopes." The song describes an ant with enormous determination, who thought he could move a big rubber tree plant and went on to make it happen.

I listened to the song over and over that very afternoon and put the rubber tree plant by my right elbow as a reminder not to give up. Within a few months, my book *Turning People On* was written and had a publisher. As of this writing, it's in its 14th printing. All because of the influence of a song, a plant, and some positive people.

If only one advisor (the ant) could give me that boost, imagine what ten positive advisors could do. Establish your Honorary Board of Advisors today and, even if the whole world lets you down (like my English prof did), you can always turn to your board for free advice. The number of people from which you can choose your advisors is virtually unlimited—historical figures, musicians, poets, writers, inventors—the list is endless. And all of the advice you will receive is FREE.

SURROUND YOURSELF WITH PEOPLE WHO HAVE BEHAVIORS, TRAITS, OR THOUGHTS THAT YOU WANT TO DEVELOP

The best way to learn Spanish is to go to a country with Spanish-speaking people and associate with them! Associate with people who act like you want to.

I noticed something very interesting about a charismatic executive of a Chicago car rental company. Not only did he have an unusual beard with no moustache, he also had unusual hand and facial mannerisms. While these aspects of his appearance were not all that interesting in themselves, what was very interesting was that some of the people working with him also had the same unusual beard and mannerisms. The employees identified with their boss. You tend to become similar to the people with whom you surround yourself.

Did you ever find yourself imitating the mannerisms, the speech, or the vocabulary of others? Currently, I am in Wetaskiwin, Alberta. Interestingly, after spending only four weeks here, I already find myself saying "eh" at the end of my sentences, a colloquialism characteristic of many Canadians. Surround yourself with people who have behavior traits and thoughts you like or admire. And even without personal effort, you will develop their characteristics.

If you want to quit smoking, make sure that you spend a great deal of time in environments of non-smokers. If you want to stop procrastinating, surround yourself with prompt, time-respecting, responsible people. And if you want to get rid of your depressions, surround yourself with positive people.

Start your Environmental Engineering Plan by (1) giving a "Cease and Desist" warning to the negative thinkers around you; (2) identifying the most positive people you know and placing them on your Board of Environmental Advisors; (3) creating an Honorary Board of Advisors from the world's most inspirational people; and (4) surrounding yourself with people who have behaviors, traits, and thoughts that you want to develop.

After putting positive people in your environment, use the second strategy in your engineering plan—overlooking the small negatives.

ENVIRONMENTAL ENGINEERING STRATEGY NO. 2: OVERLOOKING THE SMALL NEGATIVES IN YOUR ENVIRONMENT

There it was, one of the niftiest settings that your senses could bathe in. It was Easter time, and I was vacationing in one of the finest hotels on the island of Puerto Rico. Laid out for all of the guests was a huge red-velvet-covered table, featuring one of the most delectable island smorgasbords you could ever envision. Picture the delights it featured. Freshly cut steaming roast pig, lobster, clams, shrimp, and fish. Watermelons carved like bowls holding delicacies, and grapes hanging over the sides of the table as if awaiting the arrival of Cleopatra. In the background one could see the smooth-breaking Caribbean waves. The warm sea breeze was autographing the nearby palm trees. There was a Spanish guitarist playing music. A flamenco dancer waved a hello with her steps in a nearby grass hut lounge. Can you imagine the sensual setting? Could one ask for more? Well, yes. As my eyes paraded over this incredible table of delights in that magnificent setting, I overheard the woman in front of me say to her companion, "Look at this, Herman. There's a piece of over-ripe cantaloupe!"

Quite frankly, I was stopped dead in my tracks. I thought, "Things are bad, aren't they?" But after a brief pause, some good news came to me. I thought, "Yes, things are bad, but they could be worse . . . I could be Herman!"

Poor Herman. He was not fortunate enough to be with someone who knew how to overlook the small negatives. Instead, his friend glared herself into focus on the negative, however small, and made a mountain out of a molehill.

DID YOU EVER SEE A CLASSIFIED AD SAYING, "NITPICKERS WANTED"?

Nitpickers are a dime a dozen. And at that, they are overpaid. When conducting a THINK YOUR WAY TO SUCCESS seminar in a town outside of Detroit, one of the participants stopped me to share his experience.

"You know, it's funny," he confided, "but I can take all sorts of pressure on the job without blinking an eye. But the smallest thing in the world drives me right up the wall. It's the little things that get me the most. Is there anything I can do about dealing with the stress I put myself through because of small matters?"

"Yes," I responded, "and it is quite simple. In fact, you are already half way there just by admitting that you are putting yourself through the stress. It means you have control over, if not the event, at least your reactions to the event." I recommended a few steps to deal with small negative matters and to get success energies back on the course of the goals.

First, ask yourself if anything can be done about the matter. This point is crucial. If you determine either that (1) nothing can be done, or that (2) you choose not to use your time, monies, or energies to change the matter, then carve your decision into your BACKBONE OF REALITY (see Chapter VII, Rational Thinking to Learn to Deal with Inevitabilities). In this case, literally force yourself to change mental channels to other matters. At this point, you are way ahead of the rest of the people in the world who continue pushing a point that they either can't change or they don't want to change.

If, however, you are not sure whether you want to do something about the matter and it still bothers you, then:

1. Look at the matter in the BIG PICTURE OF YOUR LIFE. Look at the world from the sun; see the millions of stars light years away from each other. Then slowly focus in on the earth with its four-and-a-half-billion people. Look at the tens of thousands of hospital patients, the millions of cars bogged down in thousands of traffic jams, the hundreds of millions of people in serious debt, and the millions of people suffering from starvation. Again ask yourself how much bother does this matter deserve. If it still affects you then,
2. Immediately contact your friends on your advisory board and, if necessary, your Honorary Board of Advisors and ask each, "What do you think would be my best course of action?" Then,
3. ACT. Action cures worries. A Chicago doctor friend of mine, Dr. Harold Mozak tells his patients that there are two times not to worry about things. He claims that the first things not to worry about are those things that you *can't* change. So overlook those negative things that you can't change. The second group of things that my friend advises not to worry about are those things that you *can* change. There is no need to worry about this latter group either. All you have to do is change them.

Overlook the small negatives in life by placing them in the BIG PIC-TURE OF YOUR LIFE. Then decide whether you can change the small negatives and whether you want to enlist the energies necessary to change them. Then either ACT or ACCEPT. And yes, of course, always keep in mind, "Things could be worse . . . you could be Herman!"

So much for the small negatives. But what about the BIG NEGATIVES in your environment?

ENVIRONMENTAL ENGINEERING STRATEGY NO. 3: SWITCHING BIG NEGATIVES INTO POSITIVES

Like a talented photographer, develop your negatives into attractive positive prints. Hardship develops either weakness or strength, depending on the way you view and act on your negative experiences.

While talking to a friendly flight attendant on a Los Angeles-to-Chicago flight, she told me, quite casually, that she was going to lose her job as a result of an air traffic controller strike.

"You certainly don't seem upset about losing your job. Is it that you don't like the position?" I inquired.

"Oh, no, I love the work, the people, and the opportunity to fly. But it is a fact that there are fewer flights, and some people have to be laid off. And I'm in the group with the least seniority, so I'll be gone by December. But that doesn't mean my life is over. It just means my life will change. The more I think about it, the more excited I feel about the numerous other opportunities. In fact," Donna went on, "I recently overcame a bout with cancer, and I'm experimenting with new diets to see if diet can keep my cancer in check. So I've decided to apply for a scholarship to a number of dietary-oriented schools, and I'm also taking shorthand and typing courses in the evenings to brush up on my clerical skills."

Then, as the seatbelt sign flashed on announcing the preparation for landing, the inspirational bundle of warmth said to me, "You know, getting laid off may be the greatest thing that can happen to me. There's a big world of exciting things to do out there, and this fortunate event will open the doors for me."

I never saw Donna again, but now as I write about her in December, I feel joy inside of me because someone may have lost a job that she enjoyed. Why? Because she is a positive switcher!

Have you ever met any positive switchers? They can take any negative event in their environment and turn it into great results. Yet the same event could easily paralyze negative thinkers.

One of my closest friends and associates, Donald Scoleri, was an owner and manager of a few beauty and barber salons in Haddonfield, New Jersey. My intelligent and sensitive friend was everything—everything but a good business manager. Donald shared with me that he had a bachelor's and a master's degree in MIS-management. In fact, through mismanagement, he eventually lost most of his personnel. Now, understand, the average, shortsighted person would view that as a reason to give up in the beauty industry. Not Donald.

Donald went on to learn everything he could about business management. He spent time in thousands of salons trying to understand what he did wrong in his business. Today, the man who had two major business failures is one of the top practical business management lecturers in North America. Donald spends 40 to 45 weekends a year lecturing and consulting in the U.S. and Canada to salon owners. He is also co-director of People Media, Inc., in Reading, Pennsylvania, the major educational consulting firm to the beauty industry. Donald is a positive switcher.

1. *Be a positive switcher when negatives happen to you.* Like Donna, the former flight attendant, and Donald, the renowned lecturer, say to yourself, "Whatever happens to me, I will rise above the storm and turn it into a positive." Use your positive mind power.

2. *Realize that through hardship comes strength.* Remember from Chapter I that failures and successes differ not in what happens to them, but in the way they view what happens to them. Find a view that will work.

3. *When negative experiences happen to you, first see hope; second, quickly develop a positive plan; and third, act.* Get positive momentum on your side. Remember, the brightest lightning is often seen in the darkest storm.

ENVIRONMENTAL ENGINEERING STRATEGY NO. 4: INFLUENCING POSITIVELY THE ENVIRONMENT OF OTHER PEOPLE

Have you ever stopped to realize the fact that not only are other people part of your environment, but you are part of theirs? Would people select you to be a positive advisor to them? Successes are those who bring positive news and lift the spirits of others.

1. *Influence positively the environments of others by saying something positive to everyone you meet during the course of a day.* Make it a point to start off a conversation with a positive comment and to end every conversation on notes of hope and optimism.

2. *You literally create for others the type of environment that you create for yourself.* Observe two children who are creating an environment for others and watch how their behavior affects their own environment as a result.

Phaedra, age two, is always smiling and friendly to everyone. When relatives come to her house, she runs to them. As her eyes brighten, she extends her arms and says, "I love you." As you can gather, relatives love being with Phaedra. The warm feedback Phaedra gets from the people in her environment encourages her to feel that she is likeable. Because of this feeling, she smiles and extends herself even more to people.

Janette, also age two, is constantly crying and fighting and refuses to let anyone pick her up. She is a whiner and always unpleasant to everyone in her environment. When relatives come to visit her family, they tend to avoid Janette because of the way she acts toward them. Janette sends out a message to other people in her environment that she doesn't like them. They, in turn, respond by avoiding her. The feedback Janette receives from her environment is that she is unlikeable, and, consequently, she gets even more unpleasant and the vicious cycle continues.

Both Phaedra and Janette are creating environments for others in which an increased amount of what they put in returns to them. Send out positive vibes and positive vibes will come back to you.

At a seminar with insurance salespeople, I said enthusiastically to the underwriters, "There are a lot of smiles out there waiting for you," and one agent responded sarcastically, "I haven't seen any." Another agent seated up front turned around and commented on the sarcastic tone of the other agent, "And we all see why you haven't."

You create your own environment by the way you create the environment of others.

3. *Influence positively the environments of other people by being a "need recognizer."* Successful people are gracious and can spot "what is missing" or "what a person needs."

The successful director of a New York State social service agency explained why she had such positive morale in her department, despite the high "burnout" rate in the social work profession. She said, "When I am with people, I try to listen for what the person needs. For example, one of our staff members is recently divorced. This staff member's religious and family background tells me that she must be awfully lonely, because where she's from, divorce is a no-no. So, I realize that even though she doesn't request it, I must spend more time with her, helping her to see that I respect her as a human being and as an employee. Her need, I feel, is to be reassured." The director was a success, and literally increased employee productivity by influencing their lives in a positive way.

4. *Be a "what's-missing-here" type of person.* Successful salespeople see a client and immediately sense what the person needs and proceeds to fulfill the need. Successful inventors and manufacturers get a handle on "what's missing," and create something to fill the void.

Practice the "what's-missing" technique with your loved ones today. Think of your spouse, your parents, your children, or your friends, one by one. What's missing? What could they use in their lives? Think of all the possibilities—a kind word, a little affection, a dinner for two, flowers, an "I love you," or even a "Thank you." Now fill the void.

Influence positively the environments of other people by (1) saying something positive to everyone you meet; (2) creating the type of environment for people that you would like to have for yourself; (3) making yourself a need recognizer; and (4) being a "what's-missing" kind of person.

Success and a positive self-image are yours when you become part of the positive environments of others.

ENVIRONMENTAL ENGINEERING STRATEGY NO. 5: TREASURE WHAT YOU ALREADY HAVE AS PART OF YOUR LIFE

A popular song in the late 70's achieved success because of its shrewd and home-hitting lyrics. The song, written by Rupert Holmes, was called "The Piña Coláda Song." It described a man who was bored with his girlfriend and put an ad in the newspaper, seeking a girl who had similar interests to his, like drinking piña coládas and walking in the rain. He is pleased to receive a response to his ad and enthusiastically goes to meet his new friend. To his amazement, He finds that the person who responded to the ad was his former girlfriend.

Yes, he failed to treasure what he already had. He had taken her for granted and looked for greener pastures. Look at your environment. Are you taking people, your car, your home or apartment, your job, and even your life for granted? Maybe you are taking out personal ads all over the place, finding yourself restless and always thinking that the answer to life is "somewhere out there."

Relationships deteriorate because people stop working at them. Job burnout occurs because people lose that "first day" feeling about the job. And positive characteristics that people have are no longer valued because they are assumed.

1. *Look around you at everything you already have.* Things to consider might be your health, your finances, your friends, your property, and, yes, your life. Take constant inventory of the treasures that you have and count your blessings.

2. *Re-establish the power of the things that you have in your environment that can stimulate you.* Your favorite chair which comforts you

when you're weary, your favorite record that stimulates you, your fireplace that helps you to relax, your kitchen that can be a stimulus to your creativity, and even your bathtub which helps you retreat to think and soak away the pressures of the day. Take stock of what you already have in your environment.

Consider how much stress can be avoided by appreciating what you have instead of what you don't have. Watch how Mr. and Mrs. Tension differ from Mr. and Mrs. Appreciation in this matter.

Mr. and Mrs. Tension	*Mr. and Mrs. Appreciation*
"Oh, that so-and-so took that parking space. Now we'll have to walk all of that distance in this cold weather."	"That parking space is taken. But there's another one. Great. Let's get that one. It's sure great to have a car. Imagine, in the old days some people had to walk not a block, but miles and miles just to get to a market place."

Who will be better off, Mr. and Mrs. Tension or Mr. and Mrs. Appreciation? The answer, of course, is obvious.

I am reminded of a very meaningful experience I had which helped me to learn the importance of treasuring what I already had. I had just finished a lecture in Vancouver, British Columbia, to psychologists on the importance of positive attitude in dealing with stress.

After the lecture, I went to a little restaurant on nearby Granville Island. Following a fine dinner, during which I reflected on the satisfying lecture I presented on positive attitudes, I walked outside and, would you believe, my day was spoiled—it was pouring! While seeing the rain, I also spotted a seriously handicapped young man selling his thin book of poetry. We conversed briefly and I bought a copy of his book and received a scribbled autograph on his work. At that moment, while proceeding to my car, I put my head down to avoid the rain.

Raymond, the handicapped young poet, seeing my head curled under my coat, proclaimed in his barely comprehensible voice, "Mister, why you look down in the rain? Look up. The rain can't kill you." And you know, he was right! Even though I had just delivered an impassioned lecture on being positive, it took a handicapped poet to help me appreciate the rain.

Try it yourself. Look up at the rain. It's part of your environment. Appreciate it. Let it help you feel alive, and consider yourself fortunate if you can walk in the rain. Raymond couldn't.

Treasure what you already have as part of your life.

ENVIRONMENTAL ENGINEERING STRATEGY NO. 6: INTELLECTUALLY STIMULATE YOURSELF BY "IDEAING-UP" YOUR ENVIRONMENT

A success environment is an environment that gives you a constant pep talk, reminds you to keep plugging away, and provides for your needs of relaxation, stimulation, meditation, and inspiration. Advertisers spend millions annually on jingles, phrases, colors, sights, and sounds that will most effectively influence buying behaviors. Why? Because it works. And creating a stimulating, positive, success-inviting environment can work for you as well if you take advantage of this multimillion dollar idea. Has a coffee commercial ever invited you to brew a cup of the advertised brand? Has a mannequin sharply decked out in a tweed ever influenced you to step into the store to look . . . and then to buy? Has a batch of freshly baked cookies ever possessed you to follow your nose to the bakery and purchase a dozen or two?

All of these stimulants were designed into your environment by the advertisers, and they influenced you to act. The advertisers successfully achieved their goals by "ideaing-up" your environment. You can accomplish your goals in a similar way by following this "ideaing-up" process and by designing your Success Environment in such a way as to motivate yourself to act.

1. *Take advantage of the multimillion dollar ideas that advertisers use by designing constant advertisements to help you succeed.* Start with the goals you designed for yourself in Chapter III. Now look at your home or work environment, and design it in a way to help you reach your goals. Take the goal, "I want to lose 20 pounds," for example. As Director of Environmental Engineering, hire yourself an advertiser to promote the achievement of this goal. Set up an Environmental Design Plan and include as many stimulating ideas and reminders as you can.

Put up a sign on your refrigerator which reads, NO HIGH CALORIE FOODS PERMITTED IN THIS AREA.

Add a few pictures of trim people around this sign on your refrigerator.

Buy a scale and weigh yourself at the same time each day.

Tape up your desired magic weight number at various conspicuous points in your house.

Assign a special room as MY EXERCISE ROOM.

Leave some environmental reminders, as YOU CAN DO IT, to inspire you to "go that extra pound."

2. *Intellectually stimulate yourself by listening to motivation and positive attitude tapes.* Listen to such inspirational speakers as Zig Zigler, Dr. Robert Schuller, Earl Nightingale, Zac Clements, W. Clement Stone, Napoleon Hill, Doug Cox, and many, many others. A regular diet of these tapes included in your environment will give you that extra boost.

3. *Read only positive motivation books.* Consider some of these following books:

Don Dinkmeyer and Lew Losoncy	*The Encouragement Book: On Becoming a Positive Person,* Prentice-Hall, Inc., Englewood Cliffs, N.J.
Napoleon Hill and W. Clement Stone	*Success Through a Positive Mental Attitude,* Hawthorne Books, New York, New York
Napoleon Hill	*Think and Grow Rich,* Wilshire Books, North Hollywood, Calif. *The Laws of Success,* Hawthorne Books, New York, New York
Henry Kirn and Lew Losoncy	*How to be Happy in Life Today, Every Day,* Encouragement Associates, West Reading, Pa.
Lew Losoncy	*Turning People On: How to Be an Encouraging Person,* Prentice-Hall, Englewood Cliffs, N.J. *You Can Do It: How to Encourage Yourself,* Prentice-Hall, Englewood Cliffs, N.J.
Maxwell Maltz	*Psycho-Cybernetics,* Wilshire Books, North Hollywood, Calif.
Og Mandino	*The Greatest Secret in the World,* Frederick Feld Publishers, Inc.
Norman Vincent Peale	*The Power of Positive Thinking,* Prentice-Hall, Englewood Cliffs, N.J.
David Schwartz	*The Magic of Thinking Big,* Wilshire Books, North Hollywood, Calif.
Monsignor Fulton J. Sheen	*Life Is Worth Living,* McGraw-Hill, New York, New York
Ben Sweetland	*I Will,* Wilshire Books, North Hollywood, Calif.

4. *When you cross paths with an inspirational quote, jot it down.* Keep the quote in a place where it will always be a reminder to you. Or better yet, memorize the quote.

My favorite quote, which I keep safely stored in my environment, is a poem written by Edgar Guest called "It Couldn't Be Done":

Somebody said: "It couldn't be done,"
    But he, with a chuckle, replied,
Well, maybe it couldn't but he would be one
    Who wouldn't say so 'til he tried.
So, he buckled right in with a trace of a grin
    On his face, if he worried he hid it.
And he started to sing as he tackled the thing
    That couldn't be done—and he did it!

Somebody scoffed: "Oh, you'll never do that,
    At least, no one has ever done it."
So he took off his coat and he took off his hat
    And the first thing we know he'd begun it.
With a bit of a grin and a lift of the chin,
    Without any doubting or quiddit,
He started to sing as he tackled the thing
    That couldn't be done and he did it.

There are thousands to tell you what cannot be done,
    There are thousands who'll prophesy failure.
There are thousands who'll point out to you one by one
    All the dangers that await to assail you.
But just buckle in with a bit of a grin,
    Just take off your coat and go to it,
And just start to sing as you tackle the thing
    That cannot be done and you'll do it.

5. *Intellectually stimulate yourself by keeping positive inspirational music to listen to before you are ready to create or make a big decision.* Consider the impact that songs make in your environment. Imagine that you are about ready to make a sales presentation to a big account and you hear the following songs:

"All we are is dust in the wind"

followed by

"We are on the eve of destruction"

followed by

"Nothing matters, and so what if it did."

Although these songs may be thought-provoking and stimulating in other situations, how would you feel, after hearing them, as you walk into a sales presentation for your account?

Now imagine that instead you heard these songs:

"High hopes, I've got high hopes"
"To dream the impossible dream"
"I've got the feeling today's the day"
"What a day this has been
    What a rare mood I'm in"
"Oh, Lord, it's hard to be humble"

How different your attitude might be if you include positive up-tempo music in your environment.

You, as Director of Environmental Engineering, can intellectually stimulate yourself by structuring your environment around the positive. Make a plan to have your home and work environment give to you the lift you need.

ENVIRONMENTAL ENGINEERING STRATEGY NO. 7: VACATION YOUR MIND AND SENSES IN NEW ENVIRONMENTS

Your mind and senses, like your body, need a vacation. And it isn't necessary for your vacation to be a dramatic fiesta in Mexico or a cruise on the Mediterranean, or even a soaking from the mist of Niagara Falls. Often, all your mind and senses really need is simply a different environment.

Psychological studies have demonstrated that human beings need environmental stimulation. Lack of stimulation can produce a dullness, an apathy towards life and sometimes even hallucinations. Children who have spent their early years of growing up in an environment lacking stimulation have shown a markedly reduced I.Q. performance, and in some cases more severe mental retardation.

The quality and variety of environments you experience has a great effect on your enthusiasm, energy, and creativity. When you arrange to have yourself experience a new environment of people, places, and things, you open up your world.

1. *Be your own travel agent and design your own free sensual vacation today.* Think for a few moments of how many places you can visit in your community that stimulate you and provide you a sense of freedom. You might include the library, the park, the river running through your city,

the airport, or the nearby woods. Remember, an important prerequisite for your vacation spot is that it must make you feel free. Develop your list and plan to give your mind and senses a stimulating vacation today.

2. *Vacation your mind and senses by planning your next holiday with something new.* If you have always vacationed at the same spot, try a new one. In your lifetime of approximately 90 vacations, why not take the special one this year and give your senses a totally new refreshing path.

3. *Vacation your mind and senses by meeting at least one new person a day.* When meeting this new person, think, "This person can teach me something if I keep an open mind." It is especially important to meet people who are different than yourself. It is a simple rule that the more a person differs from you culturally, occupationally, educationally, or even religiously, the more you can learn from that person.

4. *When choosing a place to dine, choose a new one from the routine of going to the same restaurant.* Stimulate yourself by trying new foods. Give unusual foods a chance. Try the rattlesnake salad at Dominique's in Washington, D.C., the Boston scrod at the Oyster House in Boston, the stromboli at Marty's in Reading, Pennsylvania or the Sushi Bar at the Japanese Village in Edmonton, Alberta, just for starters. Open up the yellow pages of your phone book and look at names of the smorgasbords and restaurants in your own home town. Stimulate your mind and senses by selecting a new restaurant and trying a new dish.

5. *Vacation your mind and senses by learning and using at least three new words every day.* It is a fact that the quality of your experiences is affected by the number of words you know. Words can help you to describe and experience more fully your feelings towards people, life, and the world. Some Eskimos, for example, have almost 20 different words to describe snow. Thus, they can describe snow more fully than we do. Yes, an increased vocabulary helps you to vacation your mind and senses.

Your creativity and enthusiasm are related to your environment. As Director of Environmental Engineering for yourself, vacation your mind and senses in new environments and watch your creativity and enthusiasm flow like a waterfall after a tropical rainstorm.

ENVIRONMENTAL ENGINEERING STRATEGY NO. 8: EXPOSE YOURSELF TO POSITIVE MEDIA

Just as the air you breathe affects your health system, negative media from television, radio or newspapers affects your attitude system. Wipe out the media pollution from your life. One of the easiest ways to get the wrong picture of life is to blindly accept all that you see in the media as truth. A report or story may be very one-sided.

A few years ago, I was in a midwestern city to speak at a high school graduation. On my way to the school, the inquisitive cab driver asked me what brought me into the Midwest. I explained that I was there to speak to the high school graduates about how to positively think their way to success. The cab driver slowed his car and, peering through the rear view mirror at me, sneered, "Teenagers and positive attitudes. Huh! I'll tell you about teenagers. Did you see the headlines of today's paper?" He showed me the big print which read something like, TWO BOYS CAUGHT STARTING WAREHOUSE FIRE. He added, "That's the kind of kids we have today."

Taken aback with his conclusion, I asked, "How many kids do you have in your whole city?"

"Oh, about 40,000" he said.

I responded, "40,000! Why, sir, if I were creating the headlines for the newspaper today, the same story would have read, REJOICE! 39,998 OF OUR CHILDREN NOT CAUGHT STARTING A FIRE LAST NIGHT." Yes, that's 99.99%. The headlines reflected less than 1/10,000 of the truth. The cab driver treated the headlines as though that's the way all kids are. Incredible!

I shared my experience in the cab with western Pennsylvania school superintendents and board members. One of the school superintendents, Dr. Leo Bourandas, from Butler, Pennsylvania, picked up on the idea, and a few weeks later sent me a copy of the *Butler Eagle* newspaper. The headlines read, SCHOOL SUPERINTENDENT CITES GOOD KIDS. As I went on to read the article, I was elated to see that in every category—that's right, in every single category—of discipline, 99%+ of the students had not violated the rules. I'd sure make the *Butler Eagle* my newspaper!

"I HATE THIS RADIO STATION I LISTEN TO!"

A friend of mine one time made one of the most amazing, all-time absurd statements I had ever heard. She concluded, "I hate this radio station I listen to." Just swallow that statement for a while and let it soak in. If you don't like the radio station you listen to, the answer is simple— change it. Or if you don't like the newspaper you read or the TV you watch, change it. Remember, each of these mediums has the power to influence you, and if any medium affects you negatively, it's because you have given it permission to do so.

Change the channel. Take charge of your environment by exposing yourself to positive media, and your positive attitudes will brighten your horizons.

REMIND YOURSELF DAILY TO DESIGN YOUR POSITIVE ENVIRONMENT TO WORK FOR YOU

As Director of Environmental Engineering on your own account, I hope you don't take your power lightly. Use your position well. Eliminate the pollution and influence the things that influence you. Remember the 8 Positive Strategies to Engineer Your Own Environment.

P —*P*ut positive people in your environment.
O—*O*verlook small negatives in your environment.
S —*S*witch the big negatives to positives.
I —*I*nfluence positively the environments of other people.
T —*T*reasure what you already have as part of your life.
I —*I*ntellectually stimulate yourself by "ideaing up" your environment.
V —*V*acation your mind and senses in new environments.
E —*E*xpose yourself to positive media.

You have developed your unlimited Creative Thoughts (CT), igniting them with Enthusiasm (E), and you have firmly established your Goals (G). In this chapter you've made your trip even easier by Designing a Positive Environment (DPE) in which to live. Now add to the equation your ability to be a Rational Thinker (RT) which enables you to successfully deal with the STOP signs you may meet on your path to Success City:

$$CT + E + G + DPE + RT \ldots = SUCCESS$$

CHAPTER VII

Winning Success and Happiness Through Rational Thinking

You have no doubt heard the phrase, "You are what you eat." Medical researchers find more evidence each day to support the belief that the food you eat has a powerful impact on you. If you are like most people, you find that a well-balanced diet gives you increased energy, better feelings about yourself, and approval from your M.D. at checkup time.

Yes, you are what you eat. This is exciting and powerful news. Why? Because it tells you that you have control over a very important aspect of your life, your physical well-being. Just by becoming the master of your diet, you have the freedom to select foods that will make you happier and healthier. (I'm assuming, of course, that you can say "no" to people who are trying to force you to eat something that will make you sluggish and plump.)

You are what you eat; few people would disagree. But did you know that just as you are what you eat, YOU ARE WHAT YOU THINK? Yes, the most powerful psychological revelation of the decade is the realization that your thinking creates not only your emotions, but also your actions. Behavioral research and clinical experience accumulates more evidence each day to show the relationships between your thinking and (1) your depressions, (2) your anxieties, (3) your fears, (4) your guilt, (5) your temper and other anger-related problems, (6) your feelings of failure and inferiority, and (7) your overall unhappiness and dissatisfaction in life.

Plus, the implications of your thinking don't stop with these seven emotional problems. Research supports, as well, the belief that your thinking even plays a major role in psychosomatic disorders such as (1) ulcers, (2) migraine headaches, (3) hypertension, and (4) some forms of obesity. Your thinking not only creates symptoms and unhappiness, but your thoughts are the very source of positive emotions and happiness. You are definitely what you think!

The great news is that just as you can be the master of your diet, you can be the master of your thoughts. You can be healthier and happier and more able to make your feelings and actions work for you. Can you imagine the enormous human power you have when you become master of both your physical and psychological selves through a well-balanced diet and through Rational Thinking?

This chapter focuses on how you can rid yourself of emotional problems and win success and happiness by using the powerful artillery of Rational Thinking, the greatest human weapon against unhappiness. And while the power of Rational Thinking has only recently been scientifically demonstrated, it has been advocated for over twenty centuries.

BELIEF IN RATIONAL THINKING: NOT NEW BUT SCIENTIFICALLY TRUE

Humanity has always been cognizant of the power present in the way a person looks at things. Over 2000 years ago, the stoic philosopher Epictetus argued, "No human is free who is not master of his or her thoughts." Either we are masters of our thoughts (Rational Thinking) or we are the helpless slaves to our thoughts (Irrational Thinking). Epictetus concluded, "Humans are not disturbed by things, but by the views which they take of them." The red light, the traffic jam, and the rainy weather are not negative events in themselves. Actually, they are just neutral. These events can cause no emotion, no unhappiness, no disturbance, and no ulcers. However, the things that happen to you take on meaning the very second that you give the neutral events of your life a positive or a negative balance. "This red light makes me angry," or, "I'm glad I got this red light. Now I can check this map of the city," or even, "So what if the light is red? I'll only have to stop for a few seconds." It's your view, not the color of the light that causes the emotional tension or personal frustration. The light is neither good nor bad in itself—it just is.

Epictetus, the early rational thinker, was suggesting we, as human beings, have the option of choosing how to view what happens to us in our lives. Can you remember the last time you took a neutral event and allowed it to be your master and created depression, anger, or unhappiness?

A few years following the time of Epictetus, the Roman Emperor Marcus Aurelius echoed the assertions of the early Stoic by writing, "No human is happy who does not make himself or herself so." Success and happiness are won, and they can be won by everyone regardless of what life sends their way if they use Rational Thinking.

Immanuel Kant, the 18th century philosopher, exalted the power of the way things are perceived. Kant divided human experience into two areas: (1) Noumena, or the things that are "out there" (e.g., the rainy weather, the high meat prices, the economy, etc.) and (2) Phenomena, or the things that you perceive from the noumena (e.g., this weather makes me miserable, the high meat prices give me a pain, the economy has gone down the drain, etc.). Kant proclaimed that to truly understand people, we need not look at the noumena, but at the phenomena. That is, ten people could experience the same noumena, the same life experience, but they would have ten different reactions to it. In the end, it is the way that you think about it that affects you.

The psychiatrist Alfred Adler, in my opinion the greatest practical thinker of the century, wrote about the creative power your thoughts have to overcome barriers:

> Do not forget the most important fact that neither heredity nor environment are determining factors. Both are giving only the frame and the influences which are answered by the individual in regard to his styled creative self.

What happens to us in life doesn't affect us. The view we take of the event does.

Victor Frankl, in his book *Man's Search for Meaning* (1959), wrote about his experience of being imprisoned in a war camp with apparently little chance of survival. The author described how the prison guards stripped him, scarcely fed him, and dehumanized him. Frankl concluded that the guards could do anything they wanted to do to him, and he was helpless. But the one thing they couldn't do to him was to affect the way he chose to look at his life. And, in the end, the way we view our life is what really counts. His powerful outlook gave him a strong will and kept him going, proving the power of Rational Thinking can make a person the master of any life experience.

Moorhead Kennedy, a U.S. hostage in Iran, faced death many times during his 444 days in captivity. He was awakened in the middle of many nights and told that he would be shot in the next few minutes. Each day it was a challenge just to make it to bed alive, where he wondered if he would ever see the sun again. Despite the continuous strain that he experienced, Kennedy proclaimed, "We have been through one of the toughest experiences a human could go through, and we survived pretty darn well." Kennedy went on to conclude that a great deal of good came out of a bad situation. The ex-hostage proudly asserted, "Our experiences brought the American people together, and few experiences in our lifetime could have done that." Kennedy demonstrated the power of the view you take towards what happens to you in life.

A pearl begins as an irritating grain of sand and develops into a gem. Pearls are obstacles that become opportunities. When you use the power of Rational Thinking like Frankl and Kennedy, you might string a band of pearls in your lifetime!

So we have seen the power that outlook has given human beings from the days of Epictetus up to the present time. But only recently has Rational Thinking been developed systematically so that everyone can use the same strength that Frankl, Kennedy, and most successful people use. The credit for this unparalleled discovery of Rational Thinking goes to Drs. Albert Ellis and Robert Harper. In *A New Guide to Rational Living,* the book most recommended by psychologists, the authors wrote:

> When we first began thinking and writing about rational emotive therapy in the latter half of the 1950's we could cite little research material to back up the idea that humans do not get upset, but that they upset themselves by devoutly convincing themselves of irrational beliefs about what happens to them. Since that time hundreds of experiments have clearly demonstrated that if an experimenter induces, by fair or foul means, individuals to change their thoughts, they also profoundly change their emotions and behavior. Evidence that we feel the way we think keeps accumulating, steadily reaffirmed by the work of many experimenters, including Robert Arnhein, Richard S. Lazarus, Donald Meichenbaum, Stanley Schachter and numerous others.

The research shows this point clearly. You can lead a successful and happy life by using one of the greatest gifts you have—the power of Rational Thinking.

RATIONAL THINKING: YOUR THOUGHTS CONTROL YOUR EMOTIONS AND ACTIONS

Your emotions, whether positive or negative, are a result of your thinking. And your actions, whether successful or unsuccessful, are also products of your thoughts. Consider a person who claims to have an inferiority complex. Feelings of inferiority and actions that tell of inferiority develop the second a person thinks of himself or herself as inferior. And a person's feelings of inferiority will predictably continue for as long as this person concludes, "I am inferior." But those same feelings of inferiority cease the day, the hour, the minute, and yes, the second that the person begins to see himself or herself in a new and more rational way. Consider the following way of understanding human thoughts, feelings and behavior.

Thinking or Believing	Creates	Feelings or Emotions	Which in Turn Creates	Behavior or Actions
IRRATIONAL STATEMENT				
"I am an inferior person." (Unprovable and thus irrational)		"I'm so unhappy. I'm worthless and can't do anything right. I feel horrible. I'm so inadequate."		This person doesn't take chances, gives up because of fear of failing, feelings of inadequacy. (Thus this person gets worse at things because of not trying or not developing skills.)

The moment this person concludes, "I am an inferior person," an inferiority complex is born. His emotions, actions, or inactions dance to the tune of his beliefs and his unhappiness and failure to act are a result of an irrational belief that he is inferior. Now to the key point of the chapter: How can you use these colossal powers of Rational Thinking in your everyday life to achieve success and happiness?

RATIONAL VS. IRRATIONAL THINKING: KNOW THE DIFFERENCE, FEEL THE DIFFERENCE, LIVE THE DIFFERENCE

What is irrational? Why is believing, "I am an inferior person," not provable and, as a result, irrational? The statement is an overgeneralization and is not a fact. But, remember, even though it isn't a fact, it still has a powerful effect on a person who treats it as a fact. Why isn't the comment fact? Well, because no one can possibly be an inferior person. There is no scale on which to measure the total person or conclude that one human being is inferior to another. There is no proof and thus the belief is invalid and irrational.

Now observe how we could produce a more rational and thus a more productive way of thinking. Remember, a rational statement is one that can be proven. I could say, "I am an *inferior skier* to Jean Claude Killy." Or I could even say, if it were true, "I am the most inferior skier in the whole world," and, "Every single person in the world is a superior skier to me." Even suppose that somehow or other I could, in fact, prove that every single person in the world is a more talented skier than I am. This would make me *an inferior skier* (quite rational and provable), *but* it would *not* make me *an inferior person* (irrational and unprovable). Besides, I can dance better than some; I can sing better than some; I can spell better than some; etc., etc.

Observe how rational beliefs create rational feelings and actions.

Rational Beliefs or Thoughts	Creates	Rational Feelings or Emotions	Which in Turn Creates	Rational Behaviors or Actions
"I am inferior at skiing to many other people." (Provable and thus rational)		(Enjoyment, happiness) "Because my total expertise and capabilities do not depend on just my ability to ski, I can enjoy myself and learn new skiing styles without the fear of failure."		(Heading towards Success) This person skis, finds it enjoyable because the tensions were removed. This person practices more frequently and actually improves his or her skiing ability.

BE A RATIONAL THINKER: IT'S AS EASY AS A-B-C

Now how can you make use of the systematic process of Rational Thinking to help you achieve success and happiness? You can start by learning the A-B-C's of Rational Thinking. Please take a few seconds to memorize these statements and shortly you will have the opportunity to put the system to use.

Rational Thinking

Let us deal with A and C first:

A—Activating event or experience in your life.
C—Consequent emotion that you experienced after the event.

Do you believe that events in your life cause your emotions? If so, something happens to you, e.g., failing a test (A), and you experience consequent emotion of perhaps depression (C) as a result of the event. This could be viewed as "A" causes "C". Is this formula true? You fail an exam which becomes an *A*ctivating Event "A" to cause your *C*onsequent emotion of depression "C". It does, of course, seem quite logical and rational to conclude that failing the test caused the emotion. But this formula, in actuality, is not true, and it is not rational. Let's evaluate the equation to find out whether "A" really causes "C".

To scientifically test whether failing an exam caused depression or not, we need to hypothetically try our experiment on a large cross-section of people. So let's imagine that we observed the consequent emotions of a thousand people who experienced the same failure. If all 1000 people reacted exactly the same way to "A" with feelings of unhappiness, sadness, or depression, then we could conclude that "A" appears to cause "C".

Well, in reminiscing about your days at school, you perhaps remember that different people react differently to failure. Just for hypothetical purposes, we can assume that of our sample 1000 people, some would experience the emotions of unhappiness, sadness, or depression. At the same time, however, we know from experience that a few people would become angry about the same event, while others would react as GOAL THINKERS, experiencing a brief disappointment at first, but then going ahead to develop a plan for improvement on the next exam (like studying harder). There may even be a few of the 1000 who would experience happiness at "C" because they will receive extra attention from the teacher.

Why is it that not everyone experiences the same emotions in reaction to the stimulus—the failure of the exam? The only explanation is that "A", what happens to you in life, does not cause "C", your emotions. What then does cause your consequent emotions? If we asked each of the sample group why they felt the way they did, we would learn something quite interesting. And this is the point of Rational Thinking.

From the person who was depressed, we would hear something like

"I can't stand it. This is horrible. What a catastrophe, failing the test. I'm so depressed. I'm worthless." (Not provable, thus not rational.)

From the person who was angry at "C", we might hear something like

"I'm boiling. The questions were unfair. The teacher was just trying to do me in." (Not provable, thus not rational.)

From the person who was just disappointed at "C" and went on to develop a new plan (GOAL THINKER), we would hear,

"I failed the test [a proven fact and thus rational]. That disappoints me. I'll have to work harder the next time. But I can do it. Instead of catastrophizing about the failure, I'll use my energies to get working on the next test." (Provable, and thus rational.)

So the different emotional reactions to the same stimulus demonstrate that "A" does not cause "C". "C" then must be caused by some other factor. This is where the "B" of rational thinking enters. "B" is a person's *B*eliefs or what a person tells himself or herself about the activating events "A".

Very simply, your emotions are caused by your beliefs about what happens to you, not by the original experience that activated them. Remember Victor Frankl and Moorhead Kennedy, who experienced potential overwhelming stress in their imprisoned situations? They coped because of their beliefs.

A—*A*ctivating event or experience.
B—*B*elief or what you tell yourself about the event.
C—*C*onsequent emotions.

Beliefs, not activating events, cause consequent emotions. And the wonderful news is that while you may not be in charge of what happens to you at "A", YOU ARE IN CHARGE OF THE BELIEFS YOU DEVELOP TOWARD THE EVENTS OF YOUR LIFE AT "B". IT IS YOUR BELIEFS THAT, IN THE END, CAUSE YOUR EMOTIONS. Again, remember:

YOUR RATIONAL BELIEFS	CREATE	RATIONAL EMOTIONS	CREATE	RATIONAL, SUCCESSFUL ACTIONS (Development of a plan, e.g., studying harder)

At the crux between happiness and unhappiness or between success and failure are your beliefs. Rational Thinking explains why some of your friends who appear to have everything in life are still unhappy and why some people who experience many stressful life events may be happy. It explains why a financially well-to-do person may commit suicide and an impoverished person may be the one who gives your spirits a lift. It's all in your beliefs or your view. By using these powers of Rational Thinking, you can soar above any negative life experiences.

THREE BELIEFS TO ACHIEVE SUCCESS AND HAPPINESS

(1) Have the Courage to be Imperfect.
(2) Use Your Own Stamp of Approval.
(3) Live in the Power of the Present.

Rational Thinking is using the unlimited power of your mind to live your life based on reasoning. The happiest and most successful people in the world use the A-B-C system naturally. Remember, life events at "A" do not cause your failure or unhappiness at "C". Failure and unhappiness are caused by "B", your Beliefs about what happens to you. When you change your beliefs, everything in your life changes.

If you armed yourself with these three rational beliefs, it would be impossible for you to ever again be unhappy. Memorize these three beliefs and combine them with your A-B-C system and watch the personality power you can give yourself.

THE FIRST RATIONAL BELIEF: HAVING THE COURAGE TO BE IMPERFECT

People sometimes ask me, "If there were one thing above everything else that could change my life, what would it be?" Without hesitation, I give them my answer. "The key to a successful and happy life is to have the courage to try new things, to be willing to take a risk even though you might make a mistake. Overcome one of the worst psychological diseases that humanity faces—THE DISEASE OF PERFECTIONISM!"

Psychologists point out that humans only use five to ten percent of their total potential. Imagine that! Why so little? The simple answer is that we are perfectionists. As perfectionists, we are afraid to make a mistake. We conclude that unless we are perfect, we are worthless, and the best way of protecting ourselves is not to take a chance unless we are guaranteed ahead of time that we will succeed. On the other hand, the minute we develop the courage to take a risk, we start expanding our reach into our unlimited potential.

The disease of perfectionism will be a bit difficult to conquer. But it is well worth the work. Perfectionism is the source of a whole range of afflictions. A large percentage of migraine headaches are a result of perfectionism. Many forms of ulcers, hypertension, anxiety, and depression are also related to the disease. So it will be tough, but it is well worth taking the cure. It is important to realize you are not born with the disease of perfectionism. This disease is slowly developed along the way. Allow me to share with you how experiences can invite (invite, not cause!) the onset of the disease.

THE FIRST ATTACK OF THE DISEASE OF PERFECTIONISM
(AGE 3)

Sally, age 3, wakes up with a full life. She has the courage to be imperfect, and to try something new without the fear of failure. So today she decides that she is going to be a big girl and put her own shoes on all by herself!

With full spirit, she starts working, motivated by accomplishment, success, and the reactions of Mommy and Daddy. A half hour later the tyke surmounts the Everest in her life—both shoes on her feet! With eyes as big as the Montana sky, Sally goes parading down the steps to show off her achievement. She doesn't realize that her shoes are on the wrong feet. Mom and Dad, both untreated victims of the disease of perfectionism for years, are seated at the breakfast table. They are unaware that they suffer from the disease. They only know that they are unhappy and depressed a large part of the time. Unaware of their illness, they are likewise unaware that it can be passed on, especially to young children. The excited little girl turns to Mom and Dad and points to her shoes, proclaiming, "Look what I did!" Feel her life? At this moment, Sally is tapping perhaps 90% instead of only 10% of her potential because she does not suffer from the disease of perfectionism. Feel her sense of lift. Mom and Dad's first response is, "They're on the wrong feet." Feel it—you know the feeling because it happens every day!

Imagine how much better she would feel if the reaction from her parents was instead, "Wow, you put your own shoes on all by yourself, Sally. And you are only three. You must feel really big today. Can you show us how you did such a tough job?" (While Sally demonstrates her newfound skill, the parents can inconspicuously teach her the correct way.)

Instead, Sally grows through life with diseased thoughts like "Unless you can do something right, don't do it at all." Live a few moments fully immersed in this infectious belief and see how it can literally create tension, cause you to fear risks, and make you miserable. Couple that with some negative teachers making a big deal out of the number wrong she got instead of the number right, add the experience of Sally's coming home with a report card of four A's and one D and hearing, "Why the D?", and soon Sally succumbs to the perfectionism disease. She, like most, begins using less and less of her potential. She is now motivated not by enjoyment of the new, but rather by fear of the new because it represents potential failure.

Don't you just wish that you could, at this very moment, totally rid yourself of the disease of perfectionism and return to those days of the courageous little Sally. YOU CAN! Have what the renowned psychiatrist Rudolf Dreikurs called "the courage to be imperfect."

1. *Develop the courage to be imperfect by raising the high jump bar in your life.* One of my closest friends and top marketing consultant, Henry Kirn, lectures that he was the world's greatest high jumper. The party-loving enthusiast shouts in his lectures, "I was so good as a high jumper that in ten years of jumping, I never knocked the bar over." He turns to the lecture participants and explains, "You see, I always kept the bar at the height of one foot and could easily soar over it." After the laugh diminishes, Henry turns to the audience and challenges, "No, I am not the greatest high jumper in the world because I haven't knocked the bar off. The fact is that the greatest high jumper in the world is the one who knocks the bar over the MOST, not the LEAST. How else can you know how high you can go in life unless you keep testing your capabilities. Watch the best high jumpers. They keep at a level that challenges them. Only those suffering from the disease of perfectionism set their standards so low that they never know how high they can reach." The people of the world need you to give your best. Raise the high jump bar in your life today.

2. *Develop the courage to be imperfect by becoming improvement- and effort-oriented rather than perfection-oriented.* My friend, Howard Hafetz, the "Man of the Year" in the beauty and barbering industry in 1978, explains how he innovates. The handsome genius explains, "First, you see the need. Then you believe the need can be fulfilled. Then you hire the best people you know to fill the need. In the beginning, you discuss with them the fact that you know there will always be mistakes. But mistakes are clues to learn from. Innovation cannot take place without risks, which means mistakes are inevitable. When we find that a certain approach doesn't work, we simply look at ways to improve."

After employing the top educational consultant in the beauty industry, Joe Tammaro and Don Scoler, a genius of practical sense, the three have built People Media, Inc. into the top educational consultant business in the beauty and barbering industry. Both will admit to mistakes, but as they say, "How else can you get to the top?"

Howard has the courage to be imperfect. He is improvement and effort-oriented.

3. *Combine the courage to be imperfect with the A-B-C system of Rational Thinking.* While working with small family-owned business peo-

ple, I gave them a homework assignment that combined the power of Rational Thinking with the courage to be imperfect. I gave the following assignment to the salespeople.

a) Fully learn the A-B-C's of Rational Thinking.
b) Set a goal of sales for the week and then raise the goal like raising a high jump bar by at least 10% from the previous weeks.
c) Make the sales calls.
d) If a client says "no," realize that the activating event "A" does not cause your frustration, unhappiness, failure, or anger at "C." Only your beliefs at "B" can cause these negative and consequent emotions.
e) Change your beliefs. Make your beliefs more rational, more provable. Adopt the beliefs that all the client's "no" meant is that, at this moment, the client was not interested. Do not catastrophize. Feel good about making the effort. Analyze what you can learn from the client's "no." Improve your sales pitch to become the best you can.
f) At "B" have the courage to be imperfect. Thank your clients as Howard Hafetz, the success thinker, would.
g) With your new approach, immediately schedule another appointment.

The results were incredible. Thirty-two of the thirty-four families sold at least as much as they had the previous week. Twenty-seven of the families recorded higher sales than in their previous week and eleven of the families had their highest sales week ever.

All this success because of a combination of Rational Thinking and the courage to be imperfect. If you are presently the director of a sales force, make sure that you hire people who have the courage to be imperfect and to take a risk without the fear of failure. They and you will be well on your way to Success City.

4. *Have the courage to be imperfect by facing the fact that nobody can be perfect in everything that he or she can do.* Think of the most competent person you know. Have you ever seen this person make a mistake? If not, imagine if this person were asked to make Chinese food, climb Mt. Rainier, sing at the Kennedy Center, or drive in the Indianapolis 500 race. Would this person be NUMBER ONE and be perfect in every endeavor? With the courage to be imperfect, however, this person would always give it a fling. And as long as this person makes the effort, he or she will improve and eventually succeed.

Remember, when you sprinkle the courage to be imperfect on any experience, you not only avoid unhappiness, but you take one giant step towards your own personal success.

Next, achieve success and happiness by using your own stamp of approval.

THE SECOND RATIONAL BELIEF: USING YOUR OWN STAMP OF APPROVAL

The more negative a person's self-image is, the more the person needs the approval of other people. Simply, the relationship between self-image and approval works like this: A person who is unsure of himself or herself lacks confidence and doubts his or her own judgment or abilities and is the one who needs the stamp of approval from someone else.

"What should I wear to the party? Are you going to dress up or just wear jeans?"

"Henry asked me out on a date. I don't know whether I should go out with him or not. Should I?"

"I'm cooking a meal tonight. Does zucchini go with roast?"

You could add thousands more everyday comments to this list of self-doubting statements. Psychologists, most notably J. B. Rotter, have come to call the individuals who don't trust themselves, but instead lean on other people, as "externals." Rotter contrasted "externals" with the healthiest humans who have an "internal" point of evaluation. An "internal" person is one whose stamp of approval for behavior exists inside, not in someone else's hands.

A few years ago, Gene Wilkins, a former supervisor of mine, saw a need for a college in an eastern Pennsylvania city. The public argued and argued against this one man's thoughts. The populace concluded that there already were three colleges in Berks County, and there was no need for another. Yes, there were three colleges, but Gene Wilkins had "foursight." Sailing against the strong conservative winds that were blowing in the community at the time, Gene knew that trying to sell the idea of another college would be tough. Not a good enough reason for Gene to quit! Looking into the future, he knew of hundreds of students who had the intelligence, but not the money to attend the other three schools. Starting the new college was Gene's goal. In his first attempt to make it happen, he eventually had the decision to start the college placed on a public ballot. Election Day arrived, and the college was voted down 5 to 1 by the community of nearly 100,000 people!

How's that for an excuse to become discouraged in stepping toward a dream? Not a good enough excuse for an internal person like Gene. Discouragement was a foreign language that Gene did not understand. Instead, he drew upon his own stamp of approval, creativity, and enthusiasm, and heightened his determination. He spoke to groups and enlisted the help of some insightful future-looking public school board members and helped them to see the need.

In 1970, the eastern Pennsylvania college was formed—started by the efforts of one "internal truster" despite the opposition of thousands. In less than eight years, the college was providing education for over 12,000 people a year. The elderly, the handicapped, as well as high school valedictorians, were rubbing minds and gaining an education because of one person who trusted himself. A person with his or her own stamp of approval is a majority in any size group.

1. *Use your own stamp of approval by being an internal truster.* Each day, practice at building your self-image through trusting what you think. Every small exercise in self-trust, like allowing your mind to jog freely, slowly builds your muscles of confidence. You are the expert in your life. Have an openness to other people's ideas, but, in the end, respect your own thoughts, feelings and actions. You will then be a rare person and respect will flow in your direction. Even in the face of opposition, like Gene Wilkins, know that a person with his or her own internal trust is a majority in any size group.

2. *Face the fact that trying to live your life on every other person's approval is impossible, futile, frustrating, and, in the end, the sure road to losing respect.* Imagine that you suffer from the disease of approvalitis, and that you need everyone else's stamp of approval before you act. What would you have to do to achieve the final sense of self-satisfaction and assurance that everyone loves you?

First, pay for a printout of everyone's name and residence in the world. Next, schedule yourself to visit every country and ask every one of the 4½-billion people the questions, "Do you like me? Do you approve of every one of my actions?" Now just suppose that every single one of the 4½-billion people should say, "Yes, I like you and I approve of every single action of your whole life!"

ELECTION RESULTS

APPROVE of you   DISAPPROVE of you
4,500,000,000   0

What a finger-popping day that would be for you! Everyone in the whole wide world approved of you and every single action of your life. Your life is now set, isn't it?

No. In a matter of less than a few hours, or perhaps minutes, you would be thinking things like, "Well, that one fellow in Karachi looked like he could have gone either way on his answer," or, "I wonder if anyone in Lima, Peru, changed his or her mind since the election," or even, "What about all of the babies who were born since my survey? I don't know how they feel about me. Maybe they don't like me!"

Which would be easier—to run an approval election every day or to use your own stamp of approval? Use your energies to achieve success and happiness and watch what happens. The approval of the other people will soon become apparent as they gain respect for you.

Release yourself from the handcuffs of others today. At this moment say, "If approval comes from other people, fine; but I have all I need when I trust myself and use my own stamp of approval."

3. *Consider the approval of you by others as the icing on the cake, the extra fringe benefit, but never the cake itself.* Trust yourself and your decisions. If other people like your decisions, that is a fringe benefit and is beautiful. If they don't, that is fine, too. So, while you may like approval from other people, you don't need it. Approval from others is the icing, not the cake.

4. *Use your stamp of approval along with the A-B-C system of Rational Thinking.* If someone disapproves of you, remember your A-B-C's.

A—Activating events: someone calls your actions stupid.
B—Belief about the event:
   Rational: "While it would have been nice for the person to have liked my action, this person didn't. That's unfortunate. But my actions are owned by me. What do I think? Shall I continue on my course or shall I change? In the end, I am responsible for me. Let me trust myself."
C—Consequent Emotions:
   Disappointment, but not despair, and development of future plans.

Be a Rational Thinker by giving yourself your own stamp of approval today and watch how you gain respect from people.

After having the courage to be imperfect and using your own stamp of approval, cultivate your rational thinking ability by living in "the power of the present."

THE THIRD RATIONAL BELIEF: LIVE IN THE POWER OF THE PRESENT

How better to end a section on Rational Thinking than with a provable statement about life that I wrote for you while watching an hourglass:

The past is past,
The present is present,
Soon your present will be past,
So live in the power of the present, fast!

WINNING SUCCESS AND HAPPINESS THROUGH RATIONAL THINKING. Remind Yourself that Rational Thinking is Your Linking to Success and Happiness.

1. You are what you eat; you are what you think. Think your way to success and happiness through scientifically provable, rational thinking.

2. Your thinking creates your emotions and your actions. Rational Thinking produces rational emotions and defeats unhappiness. Rational Thinking also produces productive successful actions.

3. Build your rational muscle by practicing the A-B-C's of Rational Thinking:

A—*A*ctivating Event
B—*B*eliefs about the Event
C—*C*onsequent Emotions

Remember, your emotions are not caused by what happens to you at "A"; rather your emotion at "C" is caused by your views or Beliefs "B" about the events. Change your beliefs and you change your life.

4. Achieve success and happiness by overcoming the worst disease of humankind—PERFECTIONISM. Have the courage to be imperfect, to take risks, and to grow. Live your life out of enjoyment, not fear.

5. Achieve success and happiness by using your own stamp of approval. Waiting for everyone else's approval of your actions is like waiting to go skiing on the beaches of Acapulco. Trust yourself and you give yourself the greatest gift in the world.

6. Achieve success and happiness by living in the power of the present. Look to your right, look to your left, look up—but don't look back. You are alive at this moment. Capture it. THINK YOUR WAY TO SUCCESS AND HAPPINESS.

You have developed your self-image by unleashing your powers of creativity, igniting your enthusiasm towards your goal, designing your environment to help you achieve success easier, and developing your powers of Rational Thinking.

Now enlist the assistance of everyone you meet by developing your skills in leadership.

$$CT + E + G + DPE + RT + L + \ldots = SUCCESS$$
(Leadership)

CHAPTER VIII

Succeeding With People by Thinking Like a Leader

You can think your way to success the hard way by trying to do it by yourself. Or you can think your way to success the easy way by enlisting the aid, commitment, and involvement of everyone you know, everyone you work with, and even people you will meet today. A good policy to follow is to consider every person as being a potential missing link in your chain of success. And, surprisingly to you, you are the missing link in many other people's chains of success. In fact, the success is the one who knows what resources he or she has that others can use to achieve their own success.

It amazes me how successful people, in almost every interview I have with them, describe at least one other person who held the key that opened the opportunity door for them. Think of it! What could you, at this moment, use to make the difference in the achievement of your goals? Perhaps some words of encouragement, some personal contacts, some market insights, some finances, even some counseling? Think of some people who could provide the keys which will open your doors to a successful future. Be creative! Now enlist their involvement by learning the ways of thinking like a leader, inspiring like a leader, and having a self-image of a leader. Every social situation you engage in is a free class on How to Be a Successful Leader. Get your notebook ready.

BEGIN YOUR LEADERSHIP DEVELOPMENT PROGRAM: THE WORLD IS YOUR CLASSROOM

Observe groups of people. Find the leaders. Leaders are the ones who get things done. Leaders not only achieve their own goals, but, even more importantly, know how to help other people achieve their goals. Leaders are the rare ones who walk, talk, feel, think, and act with positive purpose. Being a leader is not a talent, as some suggest, that someone is born with. Everyday leadership courses such as the Dale Carnegie course, Leadership Effectiveness Training, and even my own *THINK YOUR WAY TO SUCCESS* programs prove that anyone can be a leader. Our experience is that when a person develops these skills in this chapter and couples them with creativity, enthusiasm, goal centering, environmental engineering, and Rational Thinking in the previous chapters, leadership develops.

Your leadership skills can be employed in every social setting. Watch how leaders act wherever you go. Be a leader watcher. As a leader watcher, you will learn that the true leader is not necessarily the one who talks the most, but is the one who keeps the group on course and keeps the drive to Success City going. You can observe leadership in operation every time two or more people get together to tackle a task.

A family sits down to make their own spaghetti noodles for the first time, and the teenage son asks the question, "What would be the best way of doing this?" The key question encourages the family members to brainstorm about each member's talents. Mom is good at mixing things the right way so could mix the dough; Susan can . . . ; Dad can . . . ; and Tim can . . . . Progress occurred because the leader asked the right question to make things happen. Each member had a purpose, a goal, a direction, rather than wandering aimlessly around the kitchen. In this instance, the teenage son's question made him a leader. Soon the family will enjoy the pasta together and each will feel a sense of accomplishment from his or her role in the task. The leader makes the difference by taking things off dead center.

A vice president of an engineering firm calls his staff of engineers together to describe a difficult task facing them. He encourages the group to think of the specific talents of each of the professionals in order to build a team to tackle the challenge. The selected members are motivated since their peers demonstrated confidence in them. The complex project is successfully completed because of the leadership skill of the vice president. The leadership style made the difference and made things move.

Yes, observe leaders in every social situation. They help to *create* solutions, *not dictate* solutions. Leaders create a successful atmosphere by raising a key question, encouraging people to recognize the talents and resources in the group members, and by motivating the group to stay on course to achieve a goal. Be a leader watcher. You will find that true leaders who last as leaders use the powerful approach of encouragement.

ENCOURAGEMENT: THE KEY INGREDIENT IN EFFECTIVE LEADERSHIP

In every group of people there are always a few people who have a positive effect on others. You know them. They are easy to be with, are interested in others, are positive and enthusiastic about life and its possibilities, and they exude a personal confidence. Because of their special talents in relating to people, they make the most effective parents, teachers, counselors, supervisors, salespeople, business people, doctors, and lawyers. Encouragement is the key ingredient in effective leadership. Never is heard a discouraging word when an encouraging leader is present!

The power of positive, encouraging leadership has only recently been recognized by the ME Theory (Management through Encouragement, Losoncy and Cahn, 1981). Formerly it was thought that the way of motivating, managing, or leading people was through bullying, telling, or using power. In fact, many books have been written which tell how to get "one up," how to intimidate, and how to win by conning (using fear, manipulation, blackmail, or even sex). In these books, any technique that one uses to win is justified. Some books even describe how to arrange the furniture in your office to intimidate, how to dress to intimidate, and how to defeat others by various other techniques. (One book goes as far as to suggest speaking to elderly people in a low hushed voice to intimidate them into thinking they are going deaf so that you can go one up!)

True leaders need no gimmicks to put other people down. Psychologists have found that people with "game playing" needs are literally lacking self-trust and confidence and thus have to create ploys to enhance their self-images. It's almost as if they are thinking, "I by myself am worthless, so I need to create phony and defensive manipulative devices."

Interestingly, let it be known that deceptive tactics are often effective in the short term. Real estate or other salespersons who make all sorts of empty short-range promises often can make a sale. But note this. The lifespan of a person's productive career in a community with that style is limited. Researchers have pointed out that word-of-mouth is the most important factor in real estate leads. Bad word-of-mouth is remembered, and soon distrust grows towards the agent, even among his peers.

Contrast that style with the leadership style of an encouraging real estate person. Larry Miller, personal friend and an outstanding real estate sales agent, tells of his sales philosophy:

> Your customers are people, not numbers. Your clients are making decisions based on your information. These decisions have a lifelong impact on them. I make it a practice to point out items of concern that they may not even be aware of. I find that building a sensitive relationship and a family feeling with my client is the only ethical way to go. My style sometimes hurts in the short run, and I occasionally lose a sale, but most of my clients do come back since they will be buying or selling again.

Larry Miller, an encourager, not only became a top salesman, but became president of the school board of a major school district in eastern Pennsylvania.

HOW TO THINK LIKE A LEADER

Start your own leadership development program now. Develop these skills that the most successful leaders in the world have and enlist the support of others by thinking like a leader. Become an encourager.

L —*L*istening with full attention.
E—*E*mpathizing with people.
A—*A*sset focusing.
D—*D*eveloping alternate perceptions.
E—*E*ncouraging team spirit.
R—*R*ecognizing the power of conveying confidence in people.

THE FIRST SKILL OF A LEADER: LISTENING WITH FULL ATTENTION

Conversation in the waiting room of a doctor's office:

1st person: (Holding her chest, obviously tense) I'm going to have my appendix removed next week. Dr. Woodly is going to do my operation.

2nd person:	(Enthused) Oh, Dr. Woodly, he's my neighbor!
3rd person:	(Looking at the second person) Well, where do you live?
2nd person:	I live on Oak Lane. (A fourth person seated within hearing distance enters the conversation.)
4th person:	Oak Lane, are you kidding? Do you know Helen Pushnik?
2nd person:	(Perks up even more) Oh, quite well. Helen's husband and my husband go golfing together!

The woman soon to be under the knife, who introduced the conversation, was totally ignored, slumped in her seat.

Does the style of this brief conversation sound familiar to you? It probably does since conversations that stray from the speaker's original concerns occur every day in almost every social and professional setting. Finding someone who is a full-attention listener is as rare as wings on a rabbit. The patient, a few days from surgery, finds no ears, only mouths, in the crowd. Her words of anxiety were mere stepping stones to everyone else's personal interests. When you hear conversations such as this one, it makes you wonder why people talk. My inspiring friend, Tom Lenich, an innovative Pennsylvania counselor, called what these people were engaged in a "shoot-and-reload-dialogue." This is when one person in a conversation talks ("shoots") while the other person is busy thinking about what he or she is going to say next ("reloads") instead of listening. Even Mark Twain observed this sort of selfish human interaction. Twain commented, "The first person in a conversation to draw a breath shall be declared the listener."

Leaders are those who are, first and foremost, effective listeners. They give full attention to the speaker's concern, feelings and theme. What a refreshing lift it is to be with someone who really listens to you and gives you the ultimate human gifts—time and attention. The listener not only gains respect and popularity in your eyes, but learns more as well. No wonder listeners become sought-after leaders.

There is a science to effective listening. Every conversation you engage in is a golden opportunity for you to build your listening skills. Through practice, the skill of effective listening will become natural to you. Listen your way to leadership.

LISTEN YOUR WAY TO THE TOP

Improve your relationships with everyone and find yourself being a leader by becoming a more effective listener. Avoid playing such games as "Can you top this?" and "Oh, that's nothing! Wait until I tell you what happened to me!" Literally change your personal relationships in one day by using these skills that leaders have in listening.

1. *Create a setting that shows the speaker that you are involved and fully attentive.* Be there! Effective listening is like dancing with the speaker's words. Smile with the humorous words, have heightened energies with the enthusiastic words, show concern with the troublesome words, and display an openness for controversial words. Practice being there!

2. *Be a fully attentive listener by making contact with your eyes.* A helpful way of showing you are present in a relationship is through your eyes. Effective listeners have an ability to use an ideal amount of eye-to-eye contact. What is ideal? Obviously, too little or no eye-to-eye contact might convey disinterest or noninvolvement. On the other hand, constant staring may be threatening and thus produce defensiveness in the speaker. The ideal amount of eye contact is the amount you feel comfortable with while avoiding frequent breaks.

In the next few interactions with people, become sensitive to the listening power in your eyes. Improve your eye contact by looking in a mirror and see what the other sees. Get in touch with the other with your eyes. Feel the encouragement power in your eyes!

3. *Be a fully attentive listener by showing your presence through your body language.* Your body posture and gestures give clues to your presence or nonpresence in a relationship. Unrelaxed or closed postures with distracting gestures tend to disrupt the easy flow of communication.

What are some of the pet annoyances (habits or mannerisms) you experience with others that stop your thought flow when speaking? Possibly yawning, looking beyond you, arms rigidly folded, stern eyebrows, frequent movements like feet bouncing, pencil tapping, etc. Practice avoiding the distancing body language gestures. Listen your way to the top by showing a relaxed, non-threatening open (arms and heart) body posture. Every single time you are with a person is an opportunity to develop your "I am here" body language.

4. *Be a fully attentive listener by sensitively unravelling the speaker's theme.* Proceed in every conversation with the thought that the speaker has a theme. The theme is not always apparent and sometimes you need to "reach into" the speaker's words. Listen unselfishly and noninterferingly to the words and, even more important, the feelings behind the words. Avoid the natural tendency to think, "How does what this person is saying affect me?" when listening.

Listening to the theme involves staying on the topic that other people start rather than introducing a new one. It also involves trying to look at the world through other people's eyes and hearing the world through other people's ears. After listening with full attention, leaders use the second skill of communication—they respond to the speaker's comments with empathy.

THE SECOND SKILL OF A LEADER: EMPATHIZING WITH PEOPLE

Have you ever found yourself caught in a conversation and you didn't know what to say next? The answer on how to respond is very simple, and you can develop your skills in responding in just a few seconds. Avoid being caught in the "mouthtrap" and make the following ideas part of your regular response style.

1. *Respond empathically and not judgmentally to the speaker's words and feelings.* You can go anywhere in the world to get a sermon or to listen to someone tell you what you should have done. But where can you find someone who will listen to you with understanding? Not many places. And that's why true leaders have the skill of empathic listening and responding. What does empathic responding involve?

First, empathic responding is listening without judging or evaluating the speaker's words. Everytime you judge "You're right" or "You're wrong," you stop the message and produce barriers that keep the full meaning from being completed. This, as you know, is frustrating for the speaker. Every day remind yourself to listen and not immediately judge the words and ideas of another. The most challenging times for you to be nonjudgmental are those occasions when your emotions and strong opinions are involved in what the speaker is saying. On this note, Carl Rogers, the psychologist who has affected the way people in families, schools, and organizations listen, wrote:

> The major barrier to mutual interpersonal communication is our very natural tendency to judge, evaluate, to approve or disapprove, the statements of the other person or group. . . . Although the tendency to make evaluations is common in almost all interchange of language, it is very much heightened in those situations where feelings and emotions are deeply involved. . . . So the stronger our feelings, the more likely it is that there will be no mutual element in communication.

> But is there any way of solving this problem, of avoiding this barrier? Real communication occurs, and this evaluative tendency is avoided, when we listen with understanding. What does this mean? It means to see the expressed idea and attitude from the other person's point of view, to sense how it feels to him, to achieve his frame of reference in regard to the thing he is talking about.

You gain an unequalled and powerful ability to lead and motivate the minute that you force yourself to hear, feel, and sense the speaker's words from the speaker's perspective.

2. *Respond empathically by turning the speaker's words into feelings.* On my first visit to Edmonton, Alberta, I received a wake-up call from a cheery Canadian prairie girl. She enlightened me with a bright, "Good morning, sir! It's seven a.m. and the temperature is zero! Have a great day." Zero outside. I panicked. An hour later in the same hotel, still not having faced the outside, I addressed a convention of the Alberta Teacher's Association and shared with the group my chilling reaction to the wake-up call.

Following the talk, a teacher of children with learning disabilities stopped me and said, "Don't let the zero temperature scare you. That's in centigrade." And like a computer she reassuringly added, "Zero degrees centigrade is equal to thirty-two degrees Fahrenheit." Two of my sweaters went off! I failed to turn the words of the wake-up girl from centigrade to Fahrenheit. So I made an inaccurate assumption. The young teacher had the ability to translate immediately one scale into another. You could say that she had empathy for my view and helped me because of it.

Leaders with empathy have the same translation talent. But instead of changing centigrade to Fahrenheit, empathic people have the ability to turn a person's words spontaneously into feelings. This ability to translate is rare indeed. Remember always the secret of listening empathically; turn words into feelings.

While delivering a motivation lecture in Des Moines, Iowa, I asked a group of about 2000 people what they would say if their first-grade son came home from school and said, "That mean teacher yelled at me in front of all the kids!" In unison, I heard 2000 people, without exception, shout, "What did you do?" And then I asked the group what the child said in response to "What did you do?", and the 2000 beautiful midwesterners declared, "Nothing." The parents' judgmental "What did you do?" yielded "nothing," literally. Communication broke down.

Now watch the power of empathic responding, of turning the child's words into feelings. Listen very carefully to these words wearing a six-year-old's ears, eyes, and heart.

"That mean teacher yelled at me in front of all the other kids."

Don't look at the words. Instead, see and hear the feelings behind the words. Look at the child's statement again and try to find at least three possible feelings. Possibly you will see embarrassment, hurt, anger, fear, or even guilt. Be a truly creative listener for feelings and find some more possible feelings. Now watch how the conversation can flow more easily by turning the words into feelings instead of judging them.

Child: That mean teacher yelled at me in front of all of the other kids.
Empathic
Parent: It sure hurts to be yelled at in front of your friends, doesn't it?
Child: (wiping his or her eyes) Yeah.
Empathic
Parent: Would you like to tell me more about it?
Child: Okay.

Success by turning a person's words into feelings. Make a plan to truly listen. First, understand instead of immediately judging people, and second, turn people's words into feelings. Now glance through this Leadership Listening Style Reminder Sheet. Keep it with you wherever you go and you will have a best friend.

HOW TO DEVELOP YOUR LEADERSHIP LISTENING STYLE

(Take one minute each morning to review this list in preparation for the day.)

Stay on their topic.
Give them attention and time.
Don't be frightened by silences.
Employ the word "you" or, even better, use their name occasionally.
Keep thinking, "What does what they are saying mean to them?" not "How does this affect me?"
Be a mirror to them—what they say is what they get.
Don't play "Can you top this?" or "That reminds me of" games.
Don't react out of your own needs.
Avoid interruptions.
When listening, don't conclude where they are going before they get there.
Think how your response will be viewed by this specific person.

Ask yourself these additional questions about what you say:

1. How does what I have said fit in with what the other person has said?
2. How does it relate to the other person's world?
3. Does it have any interest to the other person?
4. At what level have I responded to the other person's level?
5. How did what I said show the other person that he or she contributed to what I said?

6. How did what I said contribute to continuing rather than ending the conversation?
7. What does what I have said mean about you and me?
8. How honest is what I have said?
9. In what possible ways might what I have said be interpreted?
10. Did I encourage the other person by what I said?
11. How did I demonstrate that I listened to the other person?
12. Have I physically demonstrated that I've listened to the other person?
13. How did I sound? Was I enthusiastic?
14. Was the other person more encouraged or more discouraged by what I said?

Now continue your personal leadership development program by incorporating into your style the third skill of successful leaders. Asset Focusing.

THE THIRD SKILL OF A LEADER: ASSET FOCUSING

Besides listening with full attention and empathizing with people, another essential skill in leadership is being able to spotlight and magnify an individual's strength, assets, and resources. We all know people who are nitpickers and flaw-finders, who focus in on spotting a mistake, a weakness, or something which isn't as it "should" be. They are often quick to offer criticism. Be an individual who is finely tuned to hearing and seeing assets.

1. *Develop your skills in Asset Focusing by conditioning yourself to immediately zero in on the assets in people you meet.* I often watch what I consider to be the greatest encourager in the world—my father. After retiring from his regular work, Dad was so popular he was elected constable in his community. A constable, as you know, serves warrants and takes law breakers to prison, court, etc., a quite difficult and not very rewarding job, one might think. Not true for my father. He loves his work and rarely ever has a problem in eliciting the cooperation of the offenders. What is his secret of success?

Simple. The common sense psychologist (who has never taken a psychology course) humbly explains, "My job is to get people to cooperate. So when I visit people's homes with a warrant, I start by imagining I am in their shoes. When I do that, I know if I were them, I would be anxious, try to hide, or even resist. So I'm easy, not forceful with them. I may say something like, 'I guess you feel I've come here to hassle you. I can understand your feelings.' Shortly after, I compliment them on some asset. I look for something positive and I may ask something like, 'I see you have some trophies on your fireplace. Did you win them?' After a discussion of the trophies or some other positive quality the person has, I find the person's mind open to talk. Then I tell them the details of why I am there and how it would work to their favor to cooperate rather than to live in a state of fear awaiting the next knock on the door."

If the leadership style of asset-focusing works for a person who has to break the news to people that they are under arrest, it'll work for you. Be like Dad Lew and condition yourself to see assets in the people you meet.

2. *Be a "pick-'em-up" type of person with everyone that you meet.* Grow into a leader and give people a lift by recognizing their assets. Gust Zogas, the dean of community services for an eastern U.S. college, increased evening school enrollment in his division by 300% in just two years! How did he accomplish such a task? The talented leader was an asset-focuser par excellence. Gust would personally meet every new adult seeking entry and would remember some asset the person had. Watching Gust in the college hallways is like watching a traffic policeman direct everybody to their assets. There was always a line of students waiting to speak with Gust that was similar to the Santa Claus lineup at Saks on the 24th of December. Be a real Santa Claus, like Gust, and give people the greatest gift of all—their assets—and you, like Gust, will be a sought-after successful leader.

3. *Be a leader by developing the talent of seeing people's assets even in their liabilities.* While working as a personnel consultant to a U.S. container drum company, I would analyze personnel profiles to help the company make proper placements. It was obvious that at times when the company was thinking of dismissing an employee, a further evaluation was needed. Sometimes the very liabilities of a person in one department could be seen as an asset if he were to be placed in another department. I recall the discussion I had with one stubborn employee. His compulsive style was unyielding and his inflexibility made it difficult for those who worked with him. At this same time, the company was plagued with high insurance rates due to the injuries in the plant. The plant sorely needed someone who would have the precision personality that could reverse the accident trend. "Why not put Mark in charge of safety?" the far-thinking division manager suggested.

In three years' time with Mark in charge of safety, accidents dropped 35% and so did the insurance rates. The liability of stubbornness was, to an asset-focusing leader, turned into a positive success story. In his new position, Mark proved to be a top notch employee.

Practice your skills in turning liabilities into assets. As the division manager turned the stubborn Mark into the successful Mark, let your mind flow freely and change these liabilities into assets:

Liability	Asset
Bossy	Leadership, . . .
Nosy	Curious, . . .
Socially Aggressive	
Talkative	
Fickle	
Quiet and Shy	
Daydreamer	

Think about the people around you, at home, in social settings, or on the job. Especially note the people who "drive you up the wall" the most. Be a real leader by finding the "diamond in the rough." You Can Do It!

As you train yourself to find previously neglected resources, you become not only a valuable motivator to the person, but a natural leader. Your ability to find overlooked traits helps the person to feel new value, new sparkle, new life. Even if all that everyone else sees in a person is negative, take on the challenge of seeing the person's positive characteristics. (For further information on asset-focusing, see *The Encouragement Book: On Becoming a Positive Person,* Dinkmeyer and Losoncy, 1980.)

THE FOURTH SKILL OF A LEADER: DEVELOPING YOUR ALTERNATIVE PERCEPTIONS

Was Benedict Arnold an American traitor or a British hero? Has women's liberation helped or hindered society's development? Would allowing the laws of supply and demand to regulate the economy be the best approach to a sound fiscal policy?

These questions may inspire sparks among advocates of one side or the other. And while many people fight back and forth on these issues, the true leader is one who can stand above and beyond to take a higher level perspective on the issue. While most people's responses to these questions come from their own vantage points and are steered by their own needs, the leader is one who can see the arguments of both sides objectively and provide the alternate perspectives needed.

Bud Love, the comptroller for the public trustees of Alberta, Canada, is one of the greatest masters of alternate perspective I have met. The genius of creating alternate perceptions explains how important it is to "first, listen fully to what someone is saying. Then add perspective to the ramifications to the person's comments by realizing that this person's position is coming from his or her own vantage point. Give the ideas additional credibility by adding alternate ways of perceiving the position." Bud asserts that this approach is not antagonistic, but rather "enriching." He has been quite successful with his perceptual "adding to" style.

1. *Be a leader by developing your perceptual alternatives.* You have free will and can look at people and things from many vantage points. Practice this skill constantly. As in Chapter III when you looked at a pencil in many new ways, do the same with people you know and issues that you face. Think of the last time you had a disagreement with someone. Can you stop for a minute, get into the other person's shoes, and convincingly present this person's position? If so, you take a giant step in developing your understanding and leadership style.

Glenn, a client of mine, was a very intelligent person. While I never administered any intellectual tests to Glenn, my best guess was that he was close to a genius. He had a bachelor's degree in economics and was well beyond his formal education in that discipline. Despite his ability, his education, and his awareness in economics, Glenn had difficulty finding employment. Glenn's older brother, a home builder, decided to give Glenn the position of heading a four-man sales force. Along with supervising the four men, Glenn had sales responsibilities as well. He failed miserably and was quite frustrated in this role.

In one of our counseling sessions, it became obvious why this quite knowledgeable person was not "cutting the mustard." Glenn explained, "People are so stupid that they can't see how a home fights long-range inflation. I even take my college economics books to show them. I instruct them to read the book before we meet again. Do you know that very few people ever return?" Glenn's major error was in his thinking that people perceive life as he does. All of his intelligence, his impressive background, and his knowledge actually worked against him because he didn't use it by starting off in the customer's world.

My goal was to help Glenn develop the talent of perceptual alternatives. To achieve this end, we role-played. I asked him to be a customer, and I was a skin-and-hair-care sales consultant. At the time, I was employed by a manufacturer so I was quite aware of the products and their impact on the hair and skin. Glenn became confused with the highly technical language I employed. I instructed my client to read a highly technical physiology-of-skin-care book and come back in a week to see me. At that time we would talk about what he read. Glenn got the message. He now makes it a point to remind himself every day to perceive the world from the customer's perspective. Be a leader by developing your ways of seeing things.

2. *Rise above the conflicts of your family or your organization by using perceptual alternatives.* One of the most interesting experiences I ever faced was serving as a consultant to one Pennsylvania school district. In this capacity, I had the opportunity to work with school board members, school administrators, teachers, custodians, students, and even parents. I worked with each group on "How to be Encouraging" and "How to Communicate More Effectively." The length of the sessions varied from three to 30 hours with each group.

What insights I gained! Every group in the organization had something in common. Each thought they were getting a raw deal. The board members, for example, felt they were the "unpaid scapegoats" and were basically unappreciated. The school administrators felt that they had their hands tied and couldn't make any decisions or else the boat would rock. The teachers blamed the school board for not caring, the administrators for not disciplining the students, and the children for not listening. The secondary teachers even blamed the elementary teachers for not preparing the children for high school. In turn, the elementary teachers blamed the parents for permissive child-rearing practices. The custodians criticized the administrators for not laying the law down on cleanliness in the cafeteria and hallways. The janitors blamed the teachers and students for not "picking up" in the classes. The students blamed the administration for tough, inflexible rules and accused many teachers of not caring and of being interested only in getting their paychecks. The parents blamed the school board members for using their positions as stepping stones to gain political clout, and the administrators for punishing the children when the teachers were at fault. And the parents also blamed the teachers for not teaching! Incredible, isn't it? Yet this same blaming pattern is present in every organization.

To deal with these organizational problems, I again used the technique of role-playing. I said to the teachers, "Let's imagine that we are all school administrators. We are principals, and this is a principals' convention. Now, for one-half hour, let's think about all of the things we would have to complain about." One teacher started, "Well, these teachers are always on my back to get rid of this annoying kid or that one." Another teacher chimed in, "Yes, and their parents are never satisfied. They think that their child is the only one I have in school."

On and on the problems principals face were discussed, and, as time went on, teachers walked a mile in the principal's shoes. They increased their vision and saw alternative ways of perceiving the principal's role. By rising above the conflict, it was not long before the members of the group gained appreciation for their teaching positions. They perceived the world from the alternate perspective and the grass was not greener on the other's side. Develop your leadership style by doing the same. Rise above the conflict and use perceptual alternatives.

THE FIFTH SKILL OF A LEADER: ENCOURAGING TEAM SPIRIT

1. *Build team spirit by emphasizing cooperation as opposed to competition among members.* Observe an organization, a family, or any team with flaring spirit and strong morale, and you will find a talented leader in the picture. No doubt one talent the leader possesses is a de-emphasis on competition among teammates and an accent on cooperation.

Dr. Mary Ellen Swoyer, chosen one of the 10 top teachers in the whole state of Pennsylvania, is an incredible example of a talented leader. Dr. Swoyer could take a group of the most troublesome children and soon have them working together. How? The kindergarten teacher explained, "Children are subject to many comparisons in school and at home. They hear, 'Why aren't you like your older brother?' or 'Why can't you listen like your older sister?' 'Johnny is a better baseball player than you.' 'Susie is better at math than you.' The point of the everyday experiences of most children is this competition. Emphasis on competition conveys the feeling that you are worthwhile only when you are better than someone else. As a result, children, even at age five, conclude that if they can't be better than someone else, they have to put the other person down either verbally or physically. I try to reverse the trend. I value each child for his or her own uniqueness, talents, and contributions to the class. But more importantly, I encourage cooperation. When someone is courteous, I point out to the class what I observed and ask each of the students to think of one courteous, cooperative thing he or she could do that day. It's beautiful to watch formerly uncooperative children holding doors open for each other."

Build your team spirit by focusing in on cooperation as opposed to emphasizing comparison and competition. Do as Dr. Swoyer does. Create a cooperative family feeling within the group.

2. *Build team power by giving group credit and encouraging each group member to do the same.* Talented leaders encourage the group

and they help each member to become encouragers as well. Donald Muzyka was such a talented leader. Dr. Muzyka, a divisional vice president of the Carpenter Technology Corporation, is one of the top metallurgists in the world. But besides that, Don was a leader who placed a great deal of energy in helping his five unique divisions to work together.

While listening to a lecture on Team Power with his 400 divisional employees, I was inspired by his opening remarks. The Ph.D. of metallurgy showed an acute knowledge of human behavior when he recommended, "Look at the power we have when we work together." He cited no less than five specific instances in which cooperation among the five divisions achieved successful results.

Dr. Muzyka went on to tell a story he learned from his minister on the power of teamwork. The story goes: A person was given the opportunity to observe the differences between Heaven and Hell. The person was first taken to Hell. There he observed a large banquet hall of delicious foods, yet no one could eat because their arms were extended straight out and they could not be bent to put the food into their mouths. "The frustration of hell," he thought. "You can see the things you can't have. You are immobilized."

The observer was then taken to Heaven and to his amazement he observed the same delicious food and the same unbending arms. But here, in Heaven, the people had figured out a way to eat. With their stiff arms, they faced each other and fed each other. Cooperation was the difference. It was cooperation that helped people to achieve their goals.

Cooperative, encouraging behaviors can be developed. In working with the general managers and managers of the Carpenter Technology Company over three sessions of the ME Theory-Management through Encouragement—I was amazed with the results. One manager, Bob Torcollini, commented, "I realized the power of encouragement when I saw an employee who was giving up. I worked with him, recognizing his assets and telling him about how important his contributions were to our people. He really came through."

Norman Schmitt, another manager, concluded, "It's up to us to build team morale through cooperation. If we really listen to our people, we find that they have something to say. It's up to us to recognize their efforts and to give credit to our people." Give credit, and encourage your teammates to do the same.

3. *Build team togetherness by sharing the similarities that you observe among group members.* When travelling in a foreign country, it is refreshing to meet someone from your homeland. Maybe you experienced even more of a coincidence by running into someone from your

own city when out of town. If so, perhaps you talked of common experiences, people, or restaurants. Spotting similarities is a fast, sound, effective way of building a relationship.

This skill of finding links to other people is present in effective conversationalists, good psychotherapists, and successful leaders, and it can be yours if you develop the ability to see similarities. It warms up a cold, distant relationship. There are countless potential links to make that "link-up" happen. Find the similarities.

4. *Build team togetherness by being a common interest detective.* Observe team members in your family, your church, and your social or professional organizations to find common interests. Sports, movies, cars, dancing, interior decorating, and clothing are just a few of the potential common interests to link people together. Become skilled at introducing two strangers by mentioning a subject that links them together. Because of your skill, they would be strangers for no more than a few seconds. Be a detective and find the common denominator among people.

5. *Build a person-to-person link by identifying common struggles and challenges that face each person.*

"John, you felt that way too about facing the bar exam, didn't you?

"I went bankrupt a few years ago also, and I thought I would never be in the black again. I could never have guessed that things would turn out this well."

Be a successful leader by linking people together with their common struggles and challenges.

6. *Build team togetherness by emphasizing the common goal that links the members of the team.* Members of any organization have a similar link: the achievement of the goals of that organization. An effective leader keeps pointing to that goal. To create a hard holding, strengthening link:

"This is the big game and we need the best from everyone. Guards and tackles, we need you to function as a high-powered blocking machine for our quarterback so he can get the passes off to the receivers. With everyone doing his share for the team, we can win!"

Be a winning leader by transforming a few individuals into a team through the power of linking. Look for common interests, common challenges, and common goals.

7. *Build team morale by focusing on team effort, not just success or failure.* If you think about it, success is rarely the result of one giant leap; rather, success is normally a product of a series of efforts. The people of the United States did not land a spacecraft on the moon the first day they planned the goal. No, the achievement was the result of a series of plans, trials, errors, and corrections. The effective leader knows that the most important gift that individuals can give to the team is *effort.* When people constantly give us their effort, success will eventually arrive, but if we as leaders focus only on success and failure, we may discourage the individual and soon lose the person's effort.

The encouraging leader acknowledges the efforts of team members. Any effort in itself could be considered a success. The effort is the sign of life. Effort is one of the most important resources that people have.

Judy Taylor, an outstanding kindergarten teacher, knew how to reward effort. Whenever Mrs. Taylor asked a question, she reminded her class that the only one wrong was the person who wouldn't try. All hands were raised in her class. Even if someone responded with an "incorrect" answer, he or she would be told, "I'm so glad you tried. There could be a better answer. Think quickly to find it and try again." The sensitive and warm lover of children eliminated the stigma of being wrong which leads to discouragement. Incidentally, her absentee rates were low. Any wonder!

A training specialist and my personal friend, Bill Smith, uses an innovative approach with people who are unmotivated in seeking work because of past failures in trying to secure employment. He suggests that they set a goal, such as filling out three applications a day for three straight days. If they achieve that, Bill shouts "Success." Bill emphasizes the point that it isn't important whether they are received for an interview or find employment as a result. This is oftentimes beyond their control. But what is ultimately important is that they have made an attempt, which is within their control. It was possibly through Bill's "philosophy of effort" that I decided to be a writer!

Be a "Give-it-your-best-shot" person. Like Judy Taylor and Bill Smith, encourage people to give their best effort. Instead of asking, "Did you make the swimming team?" ask, "Did you go out for the swimming team?" Instead of asking, "Did you win top honors?" ask, "Did you give it a good shot?" And do the same with your total team. Build personal and team morale by focusing in on effort, not success or failure. Success is merely a result of an effective effort; failure is merely an indication that there is a better way and, with effort, you'll find it.

8. *Emphasize the importance of improvement to team members to build realistic incentives and to "fire up" their efforts.* Help the person who failed the test to improve; assist the salesperson who had a devastating month to shoot for higher productivity; encourage the little girl who can count to three to try for four. Is there any limit to what can be achieved if a person keeps trying to do a little better today than yesterday?

Even the most effective and streamlined system in the world can be improved. Be wary of group members who want to keep things *status quo* or who fear change and improvement. Look for the person who has his eye on improvement. Keep team morale, team spirits, and team efforts high by encouraging everyone to think "Bigger and Better," "More Today than Yesterday." Be an improvement-focuser!

9. *Be a successful leader by pointing out how each person is a necessary contributor to the team goals.* The need to contribute is powerful. I'll never forget visiting a first-grade classroom when all of the children but one were outside for recess. The little lad looked at me with bright eyes and asked, "Are you the man who helps the teachers?" "Yes," I responded. "Do you know what I gotta do this week, mister? When the kids run out for recess and don't push their chairs in, I gotta be the one who does it." The little lad was enthused about his job because he was contributing.

While working as a consultant to a publishing company which had low morale in many areas, especially the stock- and order-filling departments, something interesting occurred to me. None of the employees really knew why they were there and why their contributions were significant.

I met with 33 of the clerks and stock people. I asked each of them to consider that almost every book mailed goes to an individual. This person is a human being who, perhaps like themselves, waits for the delivery each day. Each book that the stock people package each day has the potential to change lives, to change depression into joy, to change boredom to meaning in life. I congratulated them and asked that each person each day think about their contributions to the quality of people's lives!

Show group members how their unique contributions are a necessary part of the success. Show your children why they go to school. Show your trash collector why you appreciate him or her. Show mother and father how the meal they just carefully prepared is a meaningful contribution.

10. *Build team togetherness and spirit by celebrating together.* Frank Leidich was a master leader. This supervisor would celebrate a

productive season of mushroom growing by "raising the glasses of wine" with his employees. Frank had his workers rise to give themselves a standing ovation. They couldn't wait for Victory Day.

Succeed with people by thinking like a leader and tapping the wealth of power on the team.

THE SIXTH SKILL OF A LEADER: RECOGNIZING THE POWER OF CONVEYING YOUR CONFIDENCE IN PEOPLE

The philosopher Goethe argued that if you wanted someone to develop a trait, treat them as though they already had it. In their classic book, *Pygmalion in the Classroom,* the authors, Robert Rosenthal and Lenore Jacobsen, wrote, "The self-fulfilling prophecy caused people, more often than not, to perform according to your expectations." As a leader, your confidence or lack of confidence in people actually is one of the most important factors on how they will perform.

I have observed this phenomenon in numerous instances. I've seen foremen who took workers called incorrigible and turned them into productive people. I've witnessed teachers who took pupils labeled as "unteachables" and helped them to progress. Why? All because they had the power to convey their belief, "I know you can do it!"

George Vogel, the insightful director of the Council on Chemical Abuse in Berks County, Pennsylvania, is one of the top specialists in rehabilitation of drug- and alcohol-related problems. George makes no bones about the importance of finding employers who show confidence in the abilities of former drug and alcohol addicts. George explained, "One of the most crucial decisions we make in our office is to find an employer who realistically faces the disease of alcohol and drug addiction. This employer must demand responsibility from the person going through rehabilitation. And on top of that, this special employer must be one who believes that the person can be responsible. If this confidence is conveyed to the rehabilitating person, our battle is halfway won."

Dig into your own experiences to see how this leader confidence works. Did you ever have a teacher or a supervisor who didn't have confidence in you? Everything that you did was put down. The harder you tried, the more this person focused in on what went wrong. Eventually your performance level dropped; you were discouraged.

Contrarily, did you ever have a teacher, supervisor, or a leader who truly believed in your abilities and conveyed this belief to you? You were special. What happened? In this situation, you were probably more creative, less anxious, and actually proved more productive.

1. *Make a resolution every day to convey a fresh new confidence in the people around you.* Use this power of confidence by giving people a new start. Treat them as though they had the trait you wish they had—and they soon will.

2. *Be a leader by being the one person left who continues to believe in the person everyone else has given up on.* Ed Gombeda, a technical supervisor for Gilbert Associates, one of the top engineering consulting firms in the world, is amazing. His confidence in his people is overwhelming. Ed always has something positive to say about the people working for him. The manager may conclude, "Well, Tom hasn't worked out in that particular area, but with his assets I'm sure he'll succeed in this area."

Yes, the most powerful source of success or failure in the people around you is your expectations. Believe they can achieve or believe they can't; either way you'll be correct!

SUCCEEDING WITH PEOPLE BY THINKING LIKE A LEADER

Remember these leading tips:

1. Think your way to success the easy way; be a leader and enlist the help of everyone you know.

2. Observe leaders who make things happen and who achieve goals. They are encouragers, not intimidators. Be a motivator of people, not a nitpicker. Yes, encouragement is the key ingredient in effective leadership.

3. Be an encouraging LEADER:

L —*L*istening With Full Attention
E —*E*mpathizing With People
A —*A*sset-Focusing
D —*D*eveloping Your Alternative Perceptions
E —*E*ncouraging Team Spirit
R —*R*ecognizing the Power of Conveying Confidence in People

Think Like a Leader Checklist

I. Leading Through Effective Communication

   A. Develop your skills in *attending* to other people's communications.

      1. Eye-to-eye contact.
      2. A relaxed, nondistracting body posture.
      3. Staying on the topic of the conversation.
      4. Striving for 100% message transmission.

B. Develop your skills in *listening* to other people's communications.

   1. Focus on the feelings and emotions of others.
   2. Target the concerns of others.
   3. Develop the skill of nonjudgmental listening.

C. Develop your skills in *responding* to other people's communications.

   1. Use "door-openers" for further communication.
   2. Avoid "shoot-and-reload" dialogue.
   3. Respond nonjudgmentally.
   4. Demonstrate understanding of the other's message.

II. Motivating People Through Encouragement

A. Develop your *responsibility* and *productivity* skills

   1. Focus on efforts and contributions.
   2. Recognize resources, assets, and potentials.
   3. Hold people responsible without blaming them.
   4. Identify subtle and not-so-subtle ways in which people are turned off.
   5. Energize personal enthusiasm in the concerns of others.

B. Develop your *respect* for others.

   1. Convey "I have confidence in your ability."
   2. Understand the role of encourager expectation (self-fulfilling prophecy).
   3. Focus on the interests of others.
   4. Recognize people's "claims to fame."
   5. Respect people by "staying out of the way."
   6. Cooperate, not compete, with people.
   7. Build relationships with mutual respect.
   8. Recognize the value of differences and the uniqueness in people.

C. Develop your skills in identifying *similarities* and sharing these links.

D. Develop your sense of *humor* in personal relationships.

E. Develop skills in assisting others to *overcome their discouraging ideas.*

   1. Overcome negative beliefs about yourself.
   2. Overcome negative beliefs about other people.
   3. Overcome negative beliefs about the world.

F. Develop your skills in *establishing* short and long-range *goals.*

G. Develop your skills in mutually *evaluating progress* and movement toward goals.

Your formula for success is nearly complete. You have worked hard putting it all together. Now it's time for action. Get it started today! This takes us to the last skill and attitude building chapter and completes our formula for success.

CHAPTER IX

Overcoming Procrastination and Mastering the Art of Getting Started

Feel your left foot firmly planted on the third-base bag. A surge of chills runs through your body every time you think of your thrilling past accomplishment. It felt so good, hearing the solid cracking sound of your bat powerfully dispatching the pitch with laser-like accuracy over the short-stop's head off one of the league's toughest pitchers.

But you have been on this same base for what feels like ages and are getting a little bored, a bit restless. The crowd that once was standing and applauding for you is now back in its seats. Apathetic, you think to yourself, "Is that all there is? I want more." Your chin tightens in a deter-mined search for higher goals. You paint your ordinarily cautious eyes the color of courage and, as Columbus dared to look for land in the endless sea that he *knew* was there, you search in the distance for more. Your viscera tells you there is more. You spot it. There it is—a new goal, home plate, and it is calling you to claim ownership of it. Your eyes ignite your heart. As your heart warms up, your skin breaks out in chills. Your ears hear the chills shouting, "Wouldn't it be nice to be the only person in the world who could hold the deed to that next goal?" Go For It!

Your ears, finely tuned to Station W-YES, give your feet a green light to move ahead into your greatness by dashing towards your new goal. You take your bored left foot off of the third-base bag and give it life, purpose, and a reason to be. But all of a sudden, your momentum of "success-thinking" begins to decay. That negative talker inside of you listening to Station W-NO shouts, "Get back on third base, you fool. Don't you know that as long as your foot isn't hugging the bag you could get tagged out?

Stay safely on third base, and just be content that you made it this far."

You choose to listen to this discouraging accent, and with the speed of light you direct your foot to jump back on the base for safety. So you decide to stay on third base for the morning of your life . . . and time moves on.

The afternoon of your life arrives, finding you still there on the third-base bag. Your biggest thrill comes from boasting about how you made it here. But that story is getting stale. Your whole body is dressed up in a yawn. All of a sudden you are awakened by a whisper from your positive inner voice, the "success force" in you.

The exciting voice calls louder. This time your accelerating heart enthusiastically asserts, "How long are you going to sell your life to fear?" Dare to look at your goal of home base. That new goal could belong to you and could be purchased at the cost of a little personal courage.

Why not choose to develop your muscle of courage as opposed to your muscle of fear? Whichever muscle you decide at this moment to develop is the one that will grow stronger for your future challenges. Invest in your courage muscle!

You can make it home and score the run. After all, you have many assets, strengths and resources to help you. You can run fast, you can slide, but it will never happen unless you take a risk.

So your potentially life-changing dialogue ensues. Which choice will it be for you—living for new successes or dying in the stagnated water of past achievements?

Your backbone takes the shape of a question mark. Your eyes see both red and green lights, not knowing which signal to obey. All of a sudden the butterflies in your stomach unite to form a chorus and sing the song, "I'm Ready to Take a Chance Again." You open the door to your adrenalin. Your fingers "catch the success feeling." You take a lead. You increase your distance from third. You recognize that the farther you venture from base, the more anxiety you experience.

You enthusiastically turn your anxiety into fire and with the bright flame burning in your eyes, you stare at the catcher's face mask, melting it with your courage. Home plate starts giving you its lifting power. Your body states to the world, "Here I go. I'm going for it all! I'm coming home! Now!"

PROCRASTINATION IS TOUGHER THAN FACING THE CHALLENGE

If you've made it to third base, try for the run. Your next goal is much easier to attain than you may think and is, in the long run, much more fulfilling than staying on third base for life.

Charles is 20 pounds overweight, and he tells everyone that he is starting his diet. However, that same evening Charles dines with a few people, and to their amazement he orders the full course dinner. While they look at Charles with disappointment, he explains that he has decided to start his diet the next morning. Consequently, the distance to his goal will be increased. The next morning his goal will have to be 22 pounds to lose instead of 20. Plus, he will be a day older. His illogical, irrational reasoning was that it would be just as easy for him to start tomorrow. But as can easily be observed, it will be just the opposite. Each day the task becomes progressively harder. Procrastination is tougher than facing the challenge NOW.

Claudia wants to open a small card and knickknack shop since her community is lacking such a business. The goal is ideal for her. She has a great deal of creativity and merchandising skills, and she is also quite bored with her current position which allows for very little creative thinking. She tells everyone that someday she will take the leap. But right now she feels that the cost of rental space and high product costs make the venture prohibitive. So she decides to wait for the right time. She waits and watches each year how the cost of rent and cards ascends—even more than her pay raises at her position. Lo and behold, the inevitable happens. Someone else who saw the same need in the community opens up a business of the same nature. The shop is a booming success. Claudia, on the same boring, routine job, is now bitter and angry at herself for not making her move when the rent was so much lower. Yes, procrastinating is tougher in the long run than facing the challenge NOW.

Every day, Dorothy lives with anxiety, believing that something is gravely wrong with her health. She experiences every symptom in the medical books and every symptom of the diseases that she reads about in her weekly magazines. She continually complains to everyone about her problems but refuses to go to a doctor. "After the new year," "after Easter," "sometime following vacation" are her seasonal reasons for procrastinating. And each week feels more things wrong with her until she concludes that she is so bad off that nothing will help. She begins to believe that she is better off just sitting around waiting to die. Dorothy's failure to face the problem by going to her doctor causes her a daily problem of worry and anxiety that becomes almost unbearable. She fails to realize that if she finds what is wrong, it can be dealt with. She also fails to recognize that her worries can actually produce further problems. There even exists a good possibility that if she goes to a doctor, she would find the problem was just a small one. Procrastination is tougher in the long run than dealing with the problem head on IMMEDIATELY.

Michael, unemployed for three months, claims that the economy is bad and so there are no jobs available. When given a lead for employment from a friend, Lawrence thanks the person and, in the same breath, declares, "I'll have to get over there one of these days." A few weeks later, he ventures over to fill out an application for employment. The personnel specialist sadly informs him that they aren't hiring. "Well, sir, you have all of the qualifications for employment here. In fact, a few weeks ago we hired 22 new people, and you would have made an excellent candidate. But, sorry, we'll keep your name on file."

Believe me, procrastinating is tougher than facing the challenge. Go for your home-plate goal today. You will never be swifter, prices will never be lower, and your next goal will never be closer.

THE GIST OF SUCCESS: GET IT STARTED TODAY

Be a GIST person. Get It Started Today. Every single success story tells of a "magic moment," an "Aha!", or a determined "Now I'll start." And every failure has numerous tales of "I could have . . . ," or "If only . . . ," or "Someday I will . . . ." Just observe the people around you. Some are GIST people. They see a problem, they set a goal, and they proceed to Get It Started Today.

Such a GIST person is my friend, David Capasso. His remarkable success story provides an excellent example of the power of getting things started. David flunked out of high school and recalls being labeled with many negative images in school. He wandered aimlessly through life for a period of years until he decided to make something out of himself. He studied, earned a degree in barbering, and then went on to become a barber. One day, while working as a barber for a friend, he noticed his friend was struggling to run his business effectively.

"There were no books or magazines written just for barbers to tell them how to run their businesses," David's friend and employer told him. David Capasso took off his haircutting garb and proclaimed, "I am quitting."

His amazed boss turned to him and said, "What? Where are you going?"

The lad, in his early twenties, said, "I'm going to start a magazine for barbershop and hair salon owners on how to run their businesses more effectively."

"What . . . what do you know about publishing a magazine?" the owner queried.

"Nothing, but it's obvious that a magazine like this is needed, and I can learn what I need to know."

David hurried home and told his wife, "Susan, let's start a magazine." The rest is history. The so-called high school student without a future had no knowledge of the publishing business, but he had a talented, encouraging wife and a desire to Get It Started Today. Within one year, Cutter Magazine was in print. A year later Cutter boasted of having the third largest circulation of magazines in the beauty and barbering industry.

David Capasso proved that failing in high school, lacking a background in publishing, and not having an "in" are no deterrents to the person who sees a need, fires up his or her determination, and gets it started. Pick yourself up like David did, and take your first steps to success by being a GIST person. Overcome the seven major explanations for procrastination through action.

OVERCOMING PROCRASTINATION WITH GIST ACTION

What are seven major explanations or excuses used to justify waiting rather than acting? The successful GIST person can defeat any one of them. Identify your major excuse and combat it forever.

1. "I'm the kind of person who puts off things until the last minute." (Assuming the identity of a helpless procrastinator.)
2. "Not at my age." (Too young or too old.)
3. "Someday, when things change, I'll go for it." (Waits until conditions are right.)
4. "I'd probably fail if I tried." (Fear of failure.)
5. "I hate to do that." (Disinterest, boredom, routine.)
6. "I don't want to try that. I'm happy just as I am." (False contentment.)
7. "I don't have the money now." (Lack of capital.)

Excuse for Waiting	GIST Action
1. *Assuming the identity of a helpless procrastinator.* "I'm the kind of person who puts off things unti they are overdue."	1. Absurd! Even if in your past you were always late, it is inaccurate to conclude that this is the way you always will be.
	2. You will be the kind of person today that you choose to be today.
	3. Say, "I'm the kind of person who gets things done immediately." Build that identity into yourself and, like David Capasso, Get It Started!
	4. Remember, procrastination is tougher than facing the challenge!

2. *Age* (too young or too old). "I'm too young to run for political office. I need more experience."

1. If you hear this advice from someone, I can guarantee, without even knowing the speaker, that the person who tells you this is a failure. Try something. Tell a successful person of your desire to achieve some objective at a young age and you will hear something like, "Fantastic. What a great experience that would be. I respect you for your decision. Is there any way I can help you?"

2. What greater experience for a person than participating in a political campaign. Even if you go through the election process and lose (simply reread Chapter VII, Rational Thinking), you would have lessons from the loss that couldn't be bought in any schoolroom. You would be building experience for the next campaign. And imagine if you, in your youth, WIN!

3. Another way of looking at your age is that your age is actually an advantage. For example, your youth would give you a better understanding and a better empathy for the feelings of young people.

4. Read everything you can about government, politics, etc. This will not only give you background, but will help you establish credentials on your resumé.

5. Take every opportunity to speak with people of all ages to find out what they are thinking and what their needs are. Start to listen and look for solutions. Get excited about your potential contributions.

6. Read about young political success stories, people who overcame discouragement and made it.*

7. Be a GIST person. Make your plans today regardless of whether people call you too young or too old.

---

*One of the best examples I know of a success story involving a young man who decided to make a contribution to his community was that of Tom Loeper. A recent high school graduate, Tom has so much feeling for children that he ran for the school board of a major city. Barely older than some of the students for whom he would be directing policy, Tom was told time and again, "You're too young." But my friend Tom wasn't discouraged. Instead, he took advantage of the energies of his youth and plowed ahead to win. Not only did Tom win the election, but he soon found himself in the middle of the election of a new superintendent. With the votes at 4-4, Tom was to be the deciding vote. All concerned eyes in the community turned to see Tom's vote. The pressure on the young man was overwhelming, and the man called "too young" faced the decision with his conscience head on and, unintimidated, cast his vote. The new superintendent was hired. No need to say that Tom Loeper gained the respect of the citizens in the community and, as of this writing, is serving his second term. If you are ever told you are too young, remember Tom Loeper.

3. *Wait until conditions change.* "Someday I want to start an exercise program; perhaps in the summer when conditions are right."

1. If you wait for conditions to be right, you will probably wait forever, so "get on with it" today.
2. You make conditions right by getting started right in.
3. Join a health club or spa or exercise at home.
4. Consult an expert and write a program for yourself that is reasonable and realistic.
5. Encourage some other friends to join in with you.
6. Be determined to make exercise as much a part of your life as eating or sleeping.
7. When discouraged, remember the GIST principle and act. Instead of focusing on the problems of getting there or the energies that you will have to expend, focus on the great feeling you will have when finished.
8. Take pride in your self-discipline.
9. Get It Started Today.

4. *Fear of failure.* "I'd probably fail if I tried, so I might as well not try."

1. True, life has no guarantees and every time that a person tries something new, the person could fail, but . . .
2. The simple fact is that unless you change something in your life, it is unlikely that your life will get any better.
3. Should you fail, remember, never be intimidated by what you *did,* only by what you *didn't do but could have.*
4. Failure to act is the biggest failure of all. Imagine if you were in a car and decided to pass another car. While you were in the passing lane, you saw another car coming right at you. Failure to act by either going faster or going slower could lead to a catastrophe.
5. Even if you do fail, you simply correct your mistakes.
6. Wouldn't you rather fail at a young age than at an older age? Think of those areas of your life where you are procrastinating because of your fear of failure. Make a plan and Get it Started Today.

5. *Disinterest, boredom, or routine.* "I've been putting off doing the report for so long I'm just not interested in it."

1. Procrastination, in the long run, is more difficult than facing a boring or disinteresting task.
2. Every day that you don't face a task is one more day that it lingers in the back of your mind kicking up dread, anxiety, and even guilt.

3. Think to yourself, "How long a period of time do I need to accomplish this task?" Establish an approximate number of hours.
4. Without even thinking about how burdensome the task may be, quickly block out a schedule of specific hours to devote to the task.
5. Refuse to compromise these hours.
6. Build in rewards for yourself when your project is completed.
7. Experience a sense of pride. If you keep this responsible pattern going, you will be worth more money. Employers will pay extra for non-procrastinators.
8. Get It Started Today.
9. Finish the project, reward yourself, and use all of your "free" time having fun with no anxiety or guilt hanging over your head.

6. *False contentment.* "I'm happy just as I am. I don't want to change."

1. Analyze your mind. Be objectively honest with yourself. Are you really happy as you are or is that an excuse for you to procrastinate? If you conclude that you really are content, fine. Please ignore the rest of this point on false contentment. If, however, you decide that maybe you aren't quite as content as you originally thought, then proceed.
2. Question yourself about what you would like to add in your life. It is possible that if you are somewhat dissatisfied in life, it is because you have lost goals. As you remember from Chapter V, goals give you a lift because they have pulling power. Establish goals.
3. Establish a plan to reach your goals. Make sure that your plan includes specific dates, times, and places.
4. Be a GIST person. Give yourself a lift today.

7. *Lack of capital.* "I just don't have the money."

1. If you really want to start a business, you can find the capital.
2. There is a good chance that the capital will be no easier to find a year, two years, or five years from now.
3. Be creative. Make a plan and decide to set aside so many hours each day talking with realtors, bankers, economists, or financial consultants.
4. If you are a GIST person, you will find the road to your dreams.

Lick the disease that delays human progress—procrastination—by being a person who Gets It Started Today. When you do, you defeat your only opponent in life, the clock.

BEAT THE CLOCK

When you think of it, your only competitors in life are your clock and calendar. My friend Henry Kirn tells me, "I can get all of the answers in life if I have enough time." Dr. Alfred Adler, the common sense psychiatrist, knew of the value of immediate action. In one session, Adler was counseling a bright but procrastinating patient. He was encouraging her to attend college. The elder patient resisted by saying, "Oh, I don't know. I mean, if I begin college today, it will take me four whole years to finish." Adler responded, "True, and if you begin college tomorrow, it will take you four whole years and one day."

Yes, time moves on and whether we like it or not, tomorrow, next week, next month, and the next year will arrive. If you are a GIST person, you will accomplish many things by recognizing the inevitable arrival of all the tomorrows. Beat the clock. Get It Started Today.

By using the GIST principle, you not only can beat the clock, but you can achieve any goal, regardless of how large or small it is. Think big. Use the GIST principle to tackle the big one!

DON'T BE INTIMIDATED BY THE BIG PROJECT

The biggest project in the world is no bigger than the smallest project in the world. The projects of building the San Francisco Bridge, the Empire State Building, the Canadian National Tower, or the Superdome were simply a series of small projects. Even landing a man on the moon, finding a cure for polio, or cooking a twelve-course meal are all just a series of small projects.

As someone pronounced, "A journey of a thousand miles begins with the first step and progresses one step at a time." If you look at the total journey, you will become discouraged. Don't even think of the size or the distance—just take one step and off to Success City you start.

Alcoholics Anonymous gives the same advice to help people shake their drug and alcohol problems. "Don't stop drinking for the rest of your life. Just don't have a drink today." Say that to yourself each day. Any big project is just a series of small projects.

While writing my first book, I was inundated with an oceanful of comments by people who focused on the enormity of the project.

"It must take years to write a book!"

"What if you go through the whole project and still don't get a publisher?"

One student in a Rochester, New York school told me she had a goal to write a book and experienced the same discouraging advice. Her teacher spent a complete class on how difficult it was to not only write a book where one is concerned with grammar and consistency, but also on how impossible it was to get it published. Sheila told me, "So I decided against writing as a career." She went on discussing some of the content of my lecture earlier that day. She said, "In your talk, you told our class that you failed English in high school, and yet you went on to write a few books. How did you keep yourself from being discouraged?"

"Well," I explained, "the first thing I did was not listen to people who talked about how difficult it was. Instead, I sought out advice from people who were writers themselves. And second, I never looked at the project as being huge. Instead of proceeding from day one with the thought that I have to write a whole 200 pages, all I decided to do was write one page a day. Anybody—even me—could write one page a day. And one page a day is a book in less than three fourths of a year!"

Don't be intimidated by the big project. Your twelve-course meal begins with breaking open a head of lettuce; your college degree begins with going to class today; and your book involves writing one page a day. Any big project is just a series of small projects.

Get the GIST principle working for you today. No matter how far away your next goal—your home plate—appears, the run begins with a first step. Better today than tomorrow. You'll never be younger; you'll never be swifter!

ONCE YOUR DASH TOWARD HOME PLATE IS STARTED, KEEP IT GOING

Get It Started Today! Without even thinking about the goal of cleaning your house . . . act! Don't sit and look at the mess in your house and gripe at life. Get started! Pick up the first ashtray and clean it out. You're moving. When you are moving, you are taking advantage of Newton's Law. Do you remember the Law of Inertia? Newton stated that "a body in motion tends to stay in motion unless acted on by an outside force." Keep going. Keep outside forces such as negative thoughts away. Take the "ain't-no-stoppin'-me-now" approach to the task. And soon you will be sitting in your clean house or apartment inspired by its immaculate, refreshing beauty.

Be a GIST person. Get *It* Started *To*day and use the principle of inertia to keep it going. Every day is a golden opportunity to overcome procrastination and to master the art of getting started. Even in personal relationships, it is important to get started in developing an assertive style in order to have successful, healthy relationships with people. Don't procrastinate any more in your efforts to fulfill yourself in your personal relationships.

DEVELOPING HARMONIOUS FULFILLING PERSONAL RELATIONSHIPS—TODAY

Timid Tillie, Assertive Alice, and Aggressive Aggie chanced across each other while shopping. The three women were friends and decided to talk for a while. The conversation was flowing rather smoothly when Assertive Alice raised the question.

ASSERTIVE ALICE: It will soon be lunch time. Would either or both of you like to go to lunch today?

TIMID TILLIE: (shrugs shoulder) I don't know.

AGGRESSIVE AGGIE: Yes, we'll all go to Tony's for lunch.

The three girls head off to eat at Tony's. Aggressive Aggie takes over and orders three steak sandwiches.

AGGRESSIVE AGGIE: (emphatically to the waitress) Make sure they are well done!

After a short wait the three steaks arrive and the meat is rare.

WAITRESS: (handing the red steaks to the customers) Is this the way you ordered them?

TIMID TILLIE: Yes, thank you.

AGGRESSIVE AGGIE: (flings the plate across the table) You idiot! Did you hear what we ordered? And at these prices. I'm never coming back here again, and I'm going to tell all of my friends about what a rotten place this is.

ASSERTIVE ALICE: (to the waitress) No, this is not the way I prefer my steak. I would like my steak well done. Please cook this some more. Thank you.

After lunch, the three girls shop together and Aggressive Aggie continues to complain about the lunch experience for the balance of the afternoon. Timid Tillie starts whining and encourages the development of her ulcer because she "let it ride" and didn't speak up at the restaurant. But, Assertive Alice shops with 100% of her concentration unaffected by the past luncheon. Why? Because Alice was assertive rather than aggressive or timid. Assertiveness is the course of action that leads to harmonious, fulfilling personal relationships. Assertive people like Alice strive to get what they deserve while allowing other people to get what they have a right to.

1. *Stop procrastinating! Be assertive and get what you deserve beginning today.* When people break agreements with you, don't fulfill contracts with you, or invade your space, you have the right to stop them from doing so. If someone tells you how to live your life or the person in the non-smoking section of the airplane beside you smokes, you have a right to assert yourself AT THAT MOMENT! When friends say, "Let's split the dinner check" at a classy restaurant and their meals and drinks cost much more than yours, you have a right to say, "Let's look at the bill and pay for what each of us had." When the high-pressure salesperson tries to intimidate you by calling you shortsighted for not buying, you have the right to walk away. In fact, you even have the right to be shortsighted! You are not handcuffed. Consider these three styles of handling situations:

Timid (Tillie)	*Assertive* (Alice)	*Aggressive* (Aggie)
"I let everybody tread on me. I basically believe that I am less of a person, and other people are more important than me."	"I am equal to others. I will strive to get what I deserve in life without playing games with others or trying to make them be as I think they should be."	"I am more important than other people. So I am responsible to speak on their behalf."

2. *Build your assertive muscles every day by practicing getting what you deserve.* Think and act your way to assertiveness now. Don't procrastinate. Get your fair share with people. If someone is telling you what to eat, how to dress, or how to live, sensitively tell them that you'd like to decide for yourself those issues of your life that affect you. Each time you do, you will be gaining more self-respect and more respect from others.

OVERCOMING PROCRASTINATION AND MASTERING THE ART OF GETTING STARTED

Reminders

1. Today you are on third base. You can choose to stay there for the rest of your life and not take the chance of being tagged out on your way to home. However, you soon will find yourself stalemated and unfulfilled. And time moves on. Go for a new goal. Dash for home plate today.

2. Remember, staying on third base, or procrastinating, in the long run is much more difficult than facing the challenge today.

3. Take advantage of the GIST Principle. Get It Started Today.

4. Overcome the seven excuses for procrastination (identity, age, wrong conditions, fear of failure, disinterest, false contentment, and lack of capital) today by GIST ACTION.

5. Don't be intimidated by the BIG PROJECT. The BIG PROJECT is just a series of small projects. Don't think of writing the whole book. Just do one page a day, and in less than a year you will be an author.

6. Once your run toward your new goal—your home plate—is started, keep it going by using Newton's Law: A body in motion tends to stay in motion.

7. Stop procrastinating with people. Build healthy, harmonious relationships today by being assertive and getting what is rightfully yours without taking what is rightfully theirs.

CHAPTER X

Taking Up Permanent Residence on the Street of Success

Post your new address, #1 SUCCESS STREET. Move into the fine, luxurious home in a breathtaking setting overlooking the world. Feel the proud sparkling keys to your acreage dance through your fingers for the first time. Open the door, take your first step inside, and experience that "new home" feeling. You are as overwhelmed as a first-time parent as you glance at what is all yours. Yes, it's all yours and you deserve it. It fits like a Friday afternoon. And with a little funwork, you can make your residence at this prestigious address as secure as a lion's den.

Your commitment to additional funwork will make the difference because the original purchase of the land and property will not be enough to keep and improve the domicile. Thinking you will automatically continue as a success because you have read a success book is like assuming that a light bulb you put in today will last forever or thinking that cutting the grass once will assure that the grass will never be high again.

Yes, if you desire to continue to live at #1 SUCCESS STREET, you need to take a part-time fun job of building and maintaining a structurally sound positive self-image. How can you assure that your residence is kept at its best?

In the new residence housing, your positive self-image requires:

1. Your creative design and your innovative decorative arrangement (creativity).
2. An effective power and fueling system (enthusiasm).
3. Dreams and plans for the future (goals).
4. Positive neighborhood setting (environment).

5. Continual maintenance and repair work (rational thinking).
6. Budgeting of resources, people, and money to assist in your growth (your leadership).
7. Transforming your plans into action (getting started).

Yes, making your house worth even more involves part-time funwork for you. Keeping up a beautiful home doesn't work by itself. But the end product is well worth the investment, isn't it?

By the same token and even more important, building and maintaining your own positive self-image requires a little funwork each week. *Think Your Way to Success* and stay on Success Street by continually developing the seven ingredients that make up your positive self-image:

1. Creative Thinking
2. Enthusiasm
3. Goal Centering
4. Environmental Engineering
5. Rational Thinking
6. Leadership
7. Getting Started

HOW TO STAY ON #1 SUCCESS STREET

To keep self-image repair problems at a minimum and to allow your creative ideas to flow at a maximum rate, I strongly recommend this self-image maintenance and development program.

(1) Each week, preferably on a Sunday evening or Monday morning, set aside for yourself one-half hour. Consider this part-time funwork well worth the investment. Look forward to this time and consider this your special time with yourself.

(2) At the beginning of the half hour, immerse yourself in the Imagination Exercise in Chapter III on page 50. This will cleanse your mind and assist you to proceed with full throttle.

(3) Next, decide which chapter you need to review and plan to reread that chapter some day later in the week. In the meantime, put the skills, attitudes, and learnings into practice during the balance of the week.

ADDITIONAL WAYS OF STAYING ON SUCCESS STREET

1) Be determined to have a positive motivation library. Read at least one new inspirational book each month that will increase your positive attitude and that will help you to help yourself.

2) Listen to at least one positive attitude cassette each week.

3) Make a plan to attend at least two motivation lectures a year.

4) The best way to learn how to be motivated is to motivate. Be your own lecturer! Develop a pep talk and give it to yourself each day. Develop ideas that inspire you. If you would like to share your ideas with me and other readers, send them to me in care of the publisher. If you do, I may use them in a future book, giving you credit for them just as I have done in *THINK YOUR WAY TO SUCCESS.*

5) Take a few small pieces of paper that fit into your wallet or purse and

    a) on one, put the positive traits you possess to be remembered whenever you need them;

    b) on another, put your three greatest achievements to inspire you whenever you need a lift;

    c) on another, put this formula for success:
$$CT + E + G + DPE + RT + L + GS = SUCCESS$$
Memorize each letter. When you are having a problem, the answer is always in one of the letters;

    d) on another, write your physical, social, and other goals for the next 30 days (See Chapter III);

    e) on another paper, put the chapter's name in *THINK YOUR WAY TO SUCCESS* which you will reread and focus on for that week.

6) Be a GIST person. Get It Started Today. You Can Do It!

THINK YOUR WAY TO SUCCESS

You've come a long way. Achieving success is funwork. When you *THINK YOUR WAY TO SUCCESS,* you do as my friend John W. Smith, one of the world's top business management consultants, says. "You work smarter, not harder."

Whenever you have a problem refer to this book again, and you will find the answer on one of the pages. I truly hope to meet you again someday, perhaps at a THINK YOUR WAY TO SUCCESS SEMINAR. I look forward to learning from your ideas.

You deserve a reward for completing this book. Look around you at life and feel its potential through your five senses. Give yourself a standing ovation now, today, and everyday. Spread enthusiasm. The world needs you—a one percenter—to make the difference!

Keep your eyes to the skies and set your goals high. Yes, of course, I know there will be some down times for you. But when things are bad and you are discouraged, always remember that things could be worse.

In closing, I would like to share with you an inspiring note written by a student of Edison Vo-Tech School in Rochester, New York. After I spoke to the enthusiastic student body of "Inventors" at Edison, a student whom I have never had the privilege of meeting, Donna Donovan, wrote this note to every one of her fantastic classmates:

> . . . We've only one life to live and Dr. Losoncy told us yesterday that being a good person to yourself and everyone you know is what life is all about. If everybody is always good to one another, everybody is going to be happy. All ya need is love and you gotta give it to get it. We all have to think positive! No more telling yourself I can't, cause YOU CAN! You can do or be anything you set your goals at. Shoot for the highest stars, the very highest stars!

Thank you, Donna Donovan, for reminding us what, in the end, life is all about. I'd like you to be on my Board of Positive Advisors. I will never forget your words.

SHOOT FOR THE HIGHEST STARS, THE VERY HIGHEST STARS, BECAUSE THE PEOPLE OF THE WORLD NEED YOU TO BE A SUCCESS!

REFERENCES

Ansbacher, H. and Rowena. *The Individual Psychology of Alfred Adler.* New York, New York: Basic Books, 1956.

Brookover, W. B., A. Patterson and S. Thomas. "Self-Concept of Ability and School Achievement." U.S. Office of Education, Cooperative Research Project No. 845. East Lansing: Office of Research and Publications, Michigan State University.

Collins, Mary L. In *Practical Applications of Research Newsletter.* Bloomington, Indiana, June 1981.

Frankl, V. *Man's Search for Meaning.* Boston, Mass.: Beacon Press, 1959.

Dinkmeyer, D. and L. Losoncy. *The Encouragement Book: On Becoming a Positive Person.* Englewood Cliffs, N.J.: Prentice-Hall, Inc., 1980.

Ellis, A. and R. Harper. *A New Guide to Rational Living.* North Hollywood, California: Wilshire Books, 1975.

Harding, K. L. A. "A Comparative Study of Caucasian Male High School Students Who Stay in School and Those Who Drop Out." Ph.D. dissertation, Michigan State University, 1966.

Kirn, H. and L. Losoncy. *How to Be Happy in Life Today, Everyday.* West Reading, Pennsylvania: Encouragement Associates, 1982.

Lecky, P. *Self-Consistency: A Theory of Personality.* New York, New York: Island Press, 1945.

Losoncy, L. *The ME Theory: Management Through Encouragement.* West Reading, Pennsylvania: Encouragement Associates.

Losoncy, L. *Turning People On: How to Be an Encouraging Person.* Englewood Cliffs, N.J.: Prentice-Hall, Inc., 1977.

Losoncy, L. *You Can Do It: How to Encourage Yourself.* Englewood Cliffs, N.J.: Prentice-Hall, Inc., 1980.

Losoncy, L. and Richard Cahn. *School Management Through Encouragement.* West Reading, Pennsylvania: Encouragement Associates, 1982.

Maltz, M. *Psycho-Cybernetics.* North Hollywood, California: Wilshire Books, 1960.

Panati, C. *Breakthrough.* Boston, Massachusetts: Houghton-Mifflin Co., 1980.

Purkey, W. *Self-Concept and School Achievement.* Englewood Cliffs, N.J.: Prentice-Hall, Inc., 1970.

Rogers, C. R. *On Becoming a Person.* Boston, Massachusetts: Houghton-Mifflin, Inc., 1961.

Zastrow, C. *Talk to Yourself.* Englewood Cliffs, N.J.: Prentice-Hall, Inc. 1978.

Think Your Way To Success Seminars

Dr. Losoncy teaches numerous one- and two-day success seminars throughout the country during the entire year.

Should you like to receive notification of these seminars as well as a catalog of Dr. Losoncy's inspirational books and motivational cassette tapes, please write to:

Melvin Powers
SUCCESS SEMINARS
12015 Sherman Road
North Hollywood, California 91605

MELVIN POWERS SELF-IMPROVEMENT LIBRARY